Grandparenting:

IT'S NOT WHAT IT USED TO BE

Grandparenting:
IT'S NOT WHAT IT USED TO BE

EXPERT ANSWERS

TO THE QUESTIONS

GRANDPARENTS

ASK MOST

IRENE ENDICOTT

BROADMAN
&HOLMAN
PUBLISHERS

Nashville, Tennessee

Published by Broadman & Holman Publishers, Nashville, Tennessee
Acquisitions & Development Editor: Vicki Crumpton
Interior Design: Desktop Miracles, Addison, Texas
Printed in the United States of America

4262-00
0-8054-6200-7

Dewey Decimal Classification: 306.874
Subject Heading: GRANDPARENT AND CHILD
Library of Congress Card Catalog Number: 96-24113

Unattributed quotes in are my words or words from anonymous or unknown sources.

Unless otherwise noted, Scripture quotations are from the Holy Bible, New International Version, copyright © 1973, 1978, 1984 by International Bible Society. Passages marked RSV are from the Revised Standard Version of the Bible, copyrighted 1946, 1952, © 1971, 1973; TLB, The Living Bible, copyright © Tyndale House Publishers, Wheaton, Ill., 1971, used by permission; and *The Message*, the New Testament in Contemporary English, © 1993 by Eugene H. Peterson, published by NavPress, Colorado Springs, Colo.

Library of Congress Cataloging-in-Publication Data
Endicott, Irene
    Grandparenting : it's not what it used to be / Irene Endicott
        p.   cm.
    Includes bibliographical references and index.
    ISBN 0-8054-6200-7
    1. Grandparenting. 2. Grandparenting—Religious aspects.
    I. Title.
    HQ759.9.E49   1997
    306.874'5—dc20

           96-24113
           CIP

97 98 99 00 01 5 4 3 2 1

In memory of my maternal grandmother,
Alice Mae McClelland Burch (1868–1949),
mother of seventeen, grandmother of fifty-nine,
great-grandmother of forty-two,
for her legacy of love
and practical, faithful living

CONTENTS

Gloria Gaither

Today I watch my three tiny grandsons playing under the newly reconstructed grape arbor between the back door of the farmhouse and the barnyard. I push them on the sturdy rope-and-board swing that hangs from a thick branch of a maple tree near the newly planted orchard.

A few feet away, I see my husband talking to his father as I once saw his father laughing and joking with *his* father beyond the arbor where the chicken coop once stood. I see the boyish delight on my husband's face as he remembers himself as an Indiana farm kid, shy but proud that *this* is the place, his grandparents' farm, where the church youth group always gathers on Tuesday nights for fun and recreation. I hear bits of conversation as he and his father recount for the umpteenth time the hayrides through the backroads and meadows and, afterward, the singings around the piano in the parlor with Bill at the keyboard.

My own mind is full of images of my bringing three other little children here and feeling grateful that they still had their great-grandparents. I see our four-year-old, Suzanne, skipping along with her great-grandma Blanche to gather eggs in her apron from the warm nests in the brooder house. Then I see them picking grapes from the arbor on their way to the back porch, where the big, brown eggs would be wiped clean, stacked in egg cartons, and then sold fresh to friends who had not so long ago left the farm themselves to live in town.

Back to the present, I hear the sounds of a summer supper being prepared in the kitchen behind me. My daughter, Amy, and her husband, Andrew, are cooking for us tonight. I am playing with their little Lee and Suzanne's two babies, Will and Jesse, so Amy and Andrew can dish up steamed garden vegetables and healthful chicken fillets, pour the minted, iced herbal tea, and scoop fresh, unsweetened fruit into dishes that—in our less health-conscious days—once served ice cream.

Tonight it is almost as if the years between these two sets of babies have never happened. I can almost forget for a moment that Blanche and Grover Gaither–who farmed these fields, fattened the cattle, raised the chickens, canned the cherries and sweet peaches, housed all the traveling evangelists, and hosted the church fellowships and youth recreation nights–are gone. It's almost as if this house and these outbuildings never fell into disrepair, the grape arbor was never ripped out, the orchard trees never chopped to the ground, and the weeds never allowed to grow waist-high in the barn lot.

But had those passing years not threatened to erase some beautiful memories and distance our family from some important lessons, we might never have felt the urgency of restoring this place, the intrinsic value of which far outweighs its market value. Had not this place gone up for public auction, we might have kept driving by, feeling sad, reminiscing about old times, yet never getting beyond nostalgia to recognize some of the less obvious, yet more real, needs of the human heart. We might never have discovered what really sent us out here whenever our modern sophistication became stifling and our sense of human alienation—with all our crowded scheduling—left us longing for community.

We bought the homeplace back as a family project. It was a mess when we got it. There were broken water pipes, faulty electrical wiring, crumbling plaster, rotting floorboards, leaky windows, and cracked light fixtures. There was painting to be done, eaves troughs to replace, weeds to be mowed, an orchard to plant and, oh yes, a grape arbor to be rebuilt and replanted.

After the main restoration was completed, each of Grover and Blanche's granddaughters or granddaughters-in-law chose a room to decorate. Three of the great-granddaughters also took a room as their project to revive and infuse with joy, light, and a deep respect for our shared heritage.

This summer one of those great-granddaughters, her husband, and a baby boy call this place "home" on their break from graduate studies. Together our family will celebrate Will's fourth birthday here this summer. In September this place will host our large family reunion. Together, Bill Gaither and his father, George, who grew up on this farm and still lives on a part of it, will water the new trees and grapes they have planted. They may not both see the fruit from their trees, nor eat the grapes, but the children will.

All of our lives are much different from the two who first lived on this farm and built the barn to house their livestock and shelter the hay that fed them. This is the computer age, the age of information; yet with all of our information, it is here that the generations can teach us some timeless truths:

- Hearts need a home to count on.
- Individuals may be special and unique, but we are all incomplete without community.
- The seedtime and harvest, summer and winter, night and day are not just relevant to the farmer—these are the seasons of life.
- Truth is much more than fact, and wisdom greater than knowledge.
- The present cannot exist without the past; without them both, there is no future.

I am a grandmother. I am a vital link between the wisdom of the past and the uncharted territory of the future. Without this link, this generation of information will have facts, but they will not have the story.

I am also a granddaughter. I am the recipient of a heritage that cannot be lost. This generation has been called Generation X, the lost generation. The link that is my generation is fractured, self-absorbed, trying, itself, to recover. We need a Physician who is mother, father, sister, and brother. We need restoration and reconciliation with the Parent who is perfect, so that our children's children can recover their identities and reconnect to their roots.

Kids will and must be able to ask Grandmother and get not bits of pop psychology or current fad opinion but timeless truth anchored firmly in a cosmic and personal God, whose hand can be clearly seen in the story of human history. He is the Author. The story has a beginning, a continuity with plot and characters–and it will have an ending: Heaven and earth will pass away, but God's Word, His story, is eternal, and so are we all because we each have a soul. We grandparents must know the story. We must tell the story. And, most of all, we must live the story.

Acknowledgments

Thank you to Gloria Gaither for contributing the foreword. Now a grandmother of three, Gloria is living, with grace and beauty, many of the answers to the questions in this book.

I am grateful to Broadman and Holman Publishers for their confidence in me. Thanks to my editor, Vicki Crumpton, for making *Grandparenting: It's Not What It Used to Be* a clear, easy-access resource for grandparents. I appreciate her professionalism, sense of humor, and compassion for contemporary grandparents and their need for faith-based answers to grandparenting questions.

Most of all, thank you to each grandparent represented in this book. I remember you who wrote letters to the "Ask Grandmother" column in *Grandparenting* magazine. I could feel your joy and your pain as you lived this changing role in today's society.

I remember you who told me your funny stories about your grandchildren during a *Grandparenting by Grace* seminar, all of you who wrote down questions in anonymity and passed them forward because it hurt too much to say the words out loud, and those who sat with me in corners of retreat centers to ask some of the hardest questions of all.

Now, perhaps, by God's grace, the answers to your questions will touch the lives of others.

Introduction

THERE IS A FRESH BREEZE BLOWING across America. The family is coming back!

Like a nugget of gold buried under thirty-plus years of moral and spiritual decay, the American family is once again proving its resiliency as the invaluable foundation for living the good life in the twenty-first century.

In millions of families today, grandparents are playing an integral role in the transformation. We're off our rockers, providing stability, wisdom, and unconditional love to strengthen families and help them come to a sense of wholeness.

Today's changing family may consist of mom, dad, and the children, a single mom and her children, or a single dad and his children. Or grandmother and grandfather may head up a clan so mixed up they need a scorekeeper. The fifties model of mother, father, and 2.3 children is no longer the norm. But what real effect should the "norm" have inside the protective walls of an individual family?

While the media and some humanistic "experts" preach that we need to rethink the family as we have known it, many of the more than 100 million American households have moved right along, faithfully loving and caring. These are *stick-together families,* whose members hold each other up when the going gets rough. *Forgiving families,* who value each other enough to come to terms with wrong choices and painful deeds. *Tenacious families,* to whom truth, tradition, and teamwork are hallmarks of everyday living. They know that a family is what we make it, and valuable lessons can be learned from the past.

Some good things have come from the recent past. Americans are better informed today. We are moving forward instead of standing still in obsolescence. We've shed the Ozzie and Harriett stereotype in favor of a realistic look at goals and possibilities. Unlike the static Brady Bunch, today's family is recognized as a changing phenomenon that is worth preserving.

Mothers now can choose to stay at home or go to work when necessary. More men are reclaiming headship of the family, taking fatherhood seriously again. We're acknowledging the dangers of life-threatening drugs, smoking, and abuse of all kinds. Technology is keeping families together through home computers that allow flexible working hours and modems that transmit electronic family conversations on a daily basis.

Boomer generation parents and grandparents are discovering that there really *is* more to life than the here and now. They want their children and grandchildren to have a spiritual dimension in their lives, something they missed in their own upbringing. This is all quite encouraging! Family values exist in single-parent homes just as they do in the traditional nuclear family with two parents. The often maligned and misunderstood term *family values* is no longer a cliché but a reality.

The profound changes in the family, however, have been mixed blessings for today's grandparents. While standing in the gap for our children is not new, the numbers and the reasons are. Millions of children are being raised by their grandparents because, for whatever reason, their parent(s) will not or cannot do the job. Countless other thousands of grandparents are helping out in lifesaving ways. Those grandparents who find their golden years marred by repeat parenthood, lost savings, and lost dreams represent one of the saddest legacies of this century. For them, the blessing is in knowing that their grandchild is safe and will have a chance at life.

Serious problems remain. Parents need to do a better job of balancing work, church, and family. The number of child abuse reports continues to increase each year. Pervasive violence in our society has resulted in nearly thirty-nine thousand deaths by firearms between 1980 and 1991, making it the fourth highest cause of death for the time period. Gun violence is expected to continue its rise and become the highest cause of death from 1992-2002.[1] Fifty to sixty percent of first marriages end in divorce. Live-in relationships, peer pressure, media invasion, and stress[2] are but a few of the other concerns facing families including, of course, grandparents.

Apathy, cynicism and the tangible decline of civility, gentleness and kindness in America exacerbate family problems. In November 1996, William J. Bennett and other defenders of the family formed a special commission consisting of some of our nation's best nonpolitical thinkers, educators, legal minds and clergy leaders, to study the decline of these and other virtues. The work of groups such as this will, hopefully, bring America a step closer to honoring and upholding the basic institutions that have made us great: family, church, community.

You and I can help. We should not look at problems in families as issues about which we can do little or nothing. That powerless, helpless feeling dissolves when we begin to see each problem individually. It is more important than ever to know how and when to respond to family needs and outside influences. It is more important than ever to reason together as a family, to love unconditionally and accept the consequences of that love, to examine God's Word where the answers to all of life's problems have always been, and to have the courage to make a difference in the life of just one family member by our love.

It has been said that "the family is the incubator for faith. It is the matrix for teaching children such concepts as trust, honor, duty, integrity, and love. It is the environment where the fruit of the Spirit can flourish and values and virtues can take root and grow."[3]

Problems, however, will always be with us. The challenge is to confront each problem and do our best to solve it. This book contains real-life questions on almost every aspect of grandparenting plus practical, faith-based answers to help grandparents meet the challenges and enjoy the rewards of their job. The questions came from grandparents and other family members, people from many different socioeconomic levels, races, and ages. Some reflect the pure joy of grandparenting and a need to share the happiness that children and grandchildren bring into our lives. Others tell the story in vivid detail of tragedies happening in Christian families and pose questions that are easier to ask of a stranger, questions often never before spoken because of the heaviness of guilt or sorrow.

I can feel the new awakening of the family as brave questions are being asked and Bible-based answers are put to the test. I know without a doubt that because of Jesus Christ and His love for each one of us, families will grow stronger in America.

Catch the fresh breeze only beginning to blow across the land! Take it as your own, for it is a gift of grace for your family. It comes from the mouth of God.

God is at work. By His love and tender mercies, He is healing the wounds of the past and restoring the American family to a position of power and influence for the twenty-first century.

Living the Role

BECOMING A GRANDPARENT

GRANDMOTHER, GRANDFATHER

"NORMAL" GRANDPARENTING

GRANDPARENTING BY GOD'S GRACE

Living the Role

If Christ lives in us, controlling our personalities,
we will leave glorious marks on the lives we touch.
Not because of our lovely characters, but because of His.

EUGENIA PRICE[1]

BEING A GRANDPARENT HAS BEEN CALLED the best job in the world—and it is. Our parenting years behind us, we have so much fun playing with our grandchildren and watching them grow—then we get to hand them back to *their* parents. What could be better?

Grandchildren come into our lives in all sorts of ways today—by marriage, remarriage, artificial insemination, adoption, fostering, and surrogacy, to name a few. The measure of our grandparenting is not how we get them, but how well we grandparent them once they're here.

Our attitude toward this work is the key to success, even though sometimes it can be difficult to accept the timing and circumstances of the new birth. It is also important to understand our place in the family and the privilege we have to impact children's lives for Christ.

Even the best job in the world can end up different from its job description. Parents may not live up to their responsibilities, leaving grandparents with far more work than they thought came with the title and some serious questions when things don't turn out as planned. Children raised in a Christian home can grow up and take another path. Grandchildren who have been nurtured and loved can still break our hearts with their life choices.

We learn in this section how to live the role. For example, Grand-mother may see things differently from Grandfather, and that can cause friction in the best of homes. Other questions show that because daughters are different from daughters-in-law and sons of all kinds can cause unpredictable pain and loss, today's grandparents need unusual survival skills.

Even though the role of grandparent may be complicated and full of stress for many today, it's still the best job in the world. The way we live the role is critical to our success.

FACTS

- There are more than sixty million grandparents today.
- Half of all adults ages forty-five to fifty-nine are grandparents.
- Baby boomers will increase the number of grandparents to seventy-six million by 2005, an increase of 26 percent from 1992.[2]
- 94 percent of those aged sixty-plus are grandparents.
- 50 percent of those aged sixty-plus are great-grandparents.
- Today's children can expect to spend half of their lives as grandparents.[3]

Grandparents
If Only I Could Be Like Them

Life in my family is hard going and coming, switching from one family to another, always trying to satisfy both sides. But there are always heroes in a sad story, and I give this title to my grandparents.

My grandmother seems like a little angel, trying so hard to get me what I need and always having time to set me aside and just discuss different things that go on. She seems to do this with a glow that warms and refreshes my heart in ways that cannot be described. She helps the rest of the family, which lifts them into an air of loving-kindness. She cooks food that tastes so good, you hate to swallow it. I love my grandmother!

My grandfather is a man of warm nobility, a fisher, a hunter and works hard at his real job too. I look up to my grandfather as much as my dad. My grandfather is one of perfect character and joy. Just his presence seems to bring an amazing sense of knowledge and humor. He tells countless tales of humor, fact, mystery, and legend and tries to teach me everything he knows, which always comes in handy here and there. He always seems to be happy while he works and gets the best out of life. My grandfather had a variety of athletic abilities. He ran track, played tennis, football, and just about anything. He is a very relaxed man and willing to discuss anything. He helps me pull through hard times and to understand the way people are and how to react to them, such as when my other grandfather died who I loved so much.

My grandparents seem to me to be almost perfect. No people have ever helped me, loved me, or cared after me more. They come out on the top in a huge world of happiness and sadness. If only one day I could be like them!

Mark, age 13

BECOMING A GRANDPARENT

What's a Grandparent to Do?

Q. Hooray! At age sixty-two, I am finally going to be a grandparent! Our son, a vice-president of his company, married a lovely Christian girl ten years ago, both of them age thirty. They wanted children right away, especially since her biological clock was ticking. However, tests showed that conception would be difficult, if not impossible. Since that discovery, these two we love so much have been through the wringer, you might say, trying surgery and two unsuccessful in vitro fertilization experiences, which were exhausting for them mentally, emotionally, and physically. Lately she's been taking fertility drugs.

They worked! Yesterday, on her fortieth birthday, our daughter-in-law announced that in six months, she will give birth to twins! My husband and I have prayed all these years for this great news and feel doubly blessed. We are ecstatic, but we need help to be the best grandparents ever. We don't want to make any of the mistakes we have helped friends our age live through. Please help?

A. Congratulations!

Your son and his wife are typical of many contemporary couples who are waiting longer to marry and multiply.

Your children have had a particularly hard time of it. At age forty, your daughter-in-law will need your friendship during the pregnancy. Be there for her. You can do small, thoughtful things to make her daily life easier.

Now, relax about your ability to grandparent. Much of what you will do and say in your grandparenting season will come naturally, born of need and love. Start by reading *Grandparenting: It's Not What It Used to Be, Grandparenting by Grace,* and some of the resources listed in the back of each book. Then faithfully follow these six basic rules for grandparents. Write them upon the doorposts of your heart:

- Be available.
- Do not give unsolicited advice.
- Respect boundaries, yours and theirs.
- Build up. Do not tear down.
- Love as Christ loves you.
- Have fun!

Learn from the mistakes and triumphs of others, and believe me, you will have more wins than losses. Prepare yourself for the adventure of a lifetime and one of the most cherished bonds in a family. Nothing compares to the thrill of holding that first grandchild in your arms, and you'll have two firsts—one for each of you!

Enjoy every moment!

If this baby gets any cuter, I'll burst! I always heard how great this is, but I just knew I wasn't the type. How great can it be? After all, it's just a baby! But this baby is different. It's so exciting to sit and watch her be. It's better than any Broadway show or anything on TV. You just sit there and watch. Look! She's breathing! Her eyes work! And she goes home with her mother!

The sixties kids had it all wrong. Free love is grandparenting!

A New York grandmother[4]

A Love Like No Other

Q. We were presented with our very first grandchild nearly one year ago. My husband and I are fifty-four and fifty-three, respectively. Our daughter is twenty-eight. She and her husband waited to have children until both of them finished college and got their higher degrees. I read books on grandparenting, looking forward to the future. I prayed faithfully for the child to come someday. I even attended your *Grandparenting by Grace* seminar two years ago when I wasn't a grandmother. I really got ready for this, but I have to tell you that nothing—nothing—could have prepared me for the love I feel for this child.

He was born healthy and beautiful to two parents who want him and adore him and can provide for him. I got to hold him and pass him on to my husband, whose eyes were as full of tears of joy as mine were. From that moment on, I have been in love like no other feeling I've ever had before. There's something about this baby that sets him apart from all others. He's ours, and just to have the privilege of watching him grow week by week, month by month, is something for which I am eternally grateful.

He's starting to try to walk now, and his world will open wide. His grandmother and grandfather will be there, praying for and loving him.

I love him so much that I find myself going around corners to wipe away embarrassing tears of happiness. Honestly, I had no idea before he came how much he would mean to me.

A.　We read that, "If I'd only known how wonderful my grandchildren were going to be, I'd have had them first." Such clever quotes can't even come close to the indescribable love of a grandparent.

It's a love different from parental love. We are not responsible for this child. We don't have the stresses of parenting but are free to love without restriction. The helplessness about a newborn grandchild evokes in grandparents a feeling that we would, if only we could, hand-deliver this precious one to adulthood without a scrape or a scar. It is this feeling that drives everything we will say and do for the child in the years to come.

Grandparent love is born of experience, trial, and error. It's a peaceful love that helps guide a growing grandchild through the snares of a sin-sick world to a secure faith in God who is love.

Who Hath Made Thee?

Who hath made thee, little lamb?
My heart you hold in fragile hand;
Your broken bird-like "coo" and "caw"
Speak wordless mystery to awe
　　And touch my soul.

Pink-tipped fingers grip me fast
And cause cheap pleasures of the past
To wither like a worthless reed,
The offspring of self-centered greed,
　　And leave me whole.

Who could look into your face
With its sweet essences of grace,

Total trust and angelic smile
Of innocence and artless style,
    And be the same?

Surely God hath sent you here
To whisper in my earthen ear
Of heaven's purity, my goal,
Lest I should wreck his gift, my soul,
    In worldly soil.

You, a cup of water pure,
Will man pollute thee, Satan lure
Away from thy high purpose here,
And stain my joy with scalding tear?
    By my life, No!

God hath made thee, little lamb,
To walk with him on Golden Strand!
I dedicate me to that end,
And gladly, I, my life will spend
    To make it so!

Dorothy Sickal[5]

Never Say Never

Q. Our two grown children say they'll never have any children! Our son is twenty-nine, unmarried (except to his job), and our daughter says she and her husband have seen so many family problems in their friends' lives that they have soured on ever having kids of their own. Our daughter has been married five years and has had her tubes tied. To top it off, she operates a day-care center for toddlers, saying that's enough kids for her.

Where does that leave me?

A. Shortly after her marriage, my own daughter told me, "I don't want children." A year later, she was expecting and exuberant! Now she has two children. So there is always hope for you.

The one thing you can't do is force the issue. Making children uncomfortable on the subject may serve only to reinforce their current feelings. The fact is, we birth them, we raise them, we teach them, we love them, we prepare them to fly from the coop, and then, ah, then . . . they can do whatever they choose. We have no control over the circumstances or choices of our children's lives.

Where does that leave you? In a needy world, where so many children ache for love and security, the would-be grandparent who has thus far been deprived of that joy can find joy elsewhere, in other needy children.

Contact your local United Way supported agencies that help children. See if you qualify as a volunteer to read to children during their hospital stay, be a loving listener to an innocent child with HIV, perhaps even start your own day care center in your home or help at your daughter's. See if your local elementary school needs a teacher's helper a few times a week. Ask your pastor if starting a "surrogate grandparent" program in your church would be a good idea to bring "grandparentless" children together occasionally with loving senior adults.

Recently I met a caring lady like you. She had four wiggly, inquisitive toddlers in tow at a mall. None was hers by birth, and yet each one was hers in love. This was a grandmother who, by her own action, gives respite care once a week to young mothers in her neighborhood. She sought out the needy and offered her love, time, and labor for the sake of these four who obviously adored her. No one is more a grandmother than she. No children ever loved more grandly than these.

Let your grown children see that you are active in these areas. Make them proud of the "grandmother" you really are. You will fulfill your own longings and goals with your pride intact and your head held high instead of nursing self-pity and righteous indignation.

You can have the joy of grandparenting. Until your patience is rewarded with a biological grandchild, go out into the garden of life and pick your own.

> Children are a gift from God.
>
> Psalm 127:3, TLB

Whose Grandchild Is This?

Q. I've just had the second biggest shock of my life. The first one came when our son moved in with his girlfriend, telling us there would be no wedding. The second came when we were told she is pregnant. They made it clear during their bubbly, excited announcement that this baby will be our grandchild. Is it?

I tried not to let them see it, but I'm devastated! This goes against the principles and values we taught our son. My husband says there's nothing to do but accept the child when it comes and love it as our own.

A. Your husband is correct. This baby will be the child of your child and, therefore, will indeed be your grandchild.

No, this is not the way you would hope to become a grandparent, but that's not the baby's fault. Unfortunately, we parents cannot legislate the morality of our children. They will do what they please. You planted good principles and values in your son. They're still in him. Trust that, and accept what has happened for the baby's sake.

Not that you have to condone these circumstances. Your best approach is to say little, set aside your role as mother, and pick up your grandparenting armor. Put it on and concentrate on the baby. Do not lavish the mother with gifts or go along in any way with the immorality of their relationship. If you are asked how you feel, and I hope you will be, answer honestly with a great deal of love both in your voice and in your carefully chosen words. Prepare for this moment. Be ready. Your response might make the difference in your son's future, which will dramatically affect the life of your grandchild.

When the baby comes, you will begin to model Christ in the life of the child. Your compassion, acceptance, and modeling can cause your son to reflect on the values you taught him.

Remember that joy is mentioned more than two hundred times in the Bible. We are supposed to find the joy in all that comes our way. You have suffered a shock. Trust God to uncover the joy of what has happened. It begins for you with the anticipation of new life.

I'm Going to Be a What?

Q. My daughter is pregnant. She is twenty, I am thirty-nine. I raised her alone. When she moved out to get married, I was eager to resume the life I enjoyed before diapers, discipline, teenage problems, and all that goes with being a parent. That lasted six months. Now I'm going to be a *grandparent!*

I'm not ready for this!

A. Many of us have run to the mirror to check for wrinkles when we hear the blessed news. I remember that first time well, but, trust me, it gets easier after a few or a dozen. I wouldn't give up a single one of them. I am proud of every gray hair I've earned since the first one. I prefer to think of my wrinkles as laugh lines because I've had so much to be happy about all of my life.

None of us are really ready for grandparenting before the age of forty. But wait till you see that baby child! Wait till you come face-to-face with a miracle that melts into your neck, breathes ever so softly in and out against your cheek, smells as sweet as honey, and instinctively reaches out a tiny hand just for you! And this time, you're not responsible for the diapers, the discipline, or the teenage problems. All your grandbaby will want from you is your love.

You did a good job raising your girl, but your job is not yet finished. She needs you now as much as ever before. I hope you haven't told your daughter how you feel about this. You could be digging a deep chasm between the two of you. This is a time for you to rethink your purposes for living, for a look into the mirror of honest introspection to see how others really see you.

The arrival of a grandchild does not signal the end of life as you want it to be. Go ahead! Be who you want to be. While you're at it, take care of your relationship with your daughter, and prepare to fall deliriously in love at first sight with your first grandchild. Some of the happiest moments of your entire life lie ahead. Don't miss out on any of them.

Thoroughly Modern Granny

Q. The lady I work for is about fifty-three but looks younger. She has ten grandchildren, and it's like she competes with them at swimming and tennis. At the office, she loves to tell us all about how she keeps up with them.

I'm sixty-three and also a grandmother. I don't act like that. Don't you think a grandmother should act like one?

A. Younger senior executives are usually high achievers who compete tenaciously and don't give up easily. This thoroughly modern granny is enjoying who she is. There's no need for acting. I can imagine her ten grandchildren admire her greatly and have loads of fun with her just as yours do with you.

It sounds to me as though she is doing very well, with the possible exception of talking too much about her achievements. Don't begrudge her the joy she finds in this season of life. Smile and move on. I say more power to her!

Don't you think it's wonderful that each of us can have our own unique way of grandparenting?

The Mixed Race Grandchild

Q. We are a middle-class Caucasian, Christian family. My husband and I worked hard at being good parents to our only son. We've dreamed of the day he would marry and give us grandchildren to love. He's a college graduate and has dated a number of lovely girls from good families.

Last week he brought home an African-American girl who has a three-year-old son, announcing that they are expecting a child of their own and plan to be married soon. We never dreamed we'd be faced with the prospect of mixed race grandchildren. My feelings are twofold: I feel helpless to stop it, and I feel ashamed about how I reacted when they told us. I left the room and haven't talked to our son since.

A. Look at it this way: your dream has come true! You are going to get a grandchild to love, and a grandchild of mixed race is no different from a Caucasian grandchild. Every child needs all the love he or she can get. That includes the little boy coming into the family.

Contact your son. Apologize for leaving the room. Explain your shock gently and with love. Your words will be received with gratitude and relief. That's a good beginning. Then get to know your future daughter-in-law. Be kind to her. She probably needs your compassion in her present condition. Hostility toward her will damage your relationship with your son. You don't want that. There's nothing you can do to change his mind or what has happened. It's too late.

Read again Paul's definition of love in 1 Corinthians 13, and pray about each line in light of what has happened to you personally. I've always felt that one of the reasons God allows us to grow older is so that some of His wisdom will have time to sink in. Your time has come. You can do this. I know you can!

Love never gives up.
Love cares more for others than for self.

Love doesn't want what it doesn't have.
Love doesn't strut.
Doesn't have a swelled head.
Doesn't force itself on others.
Isn't always "me first."
Doesn't fly off the handle.
Doesn't keep score of the sins of others.
Doesn't revel when others grovel.
Takes pleasure in the flowering of truth.
Puts up with anything.
Trusts God always.
Always looks for the best.
Never looks back
But keeps going to the end.

1 Corinthians 13
THE MESSAGE

The Miracle Grandchild

Q. We had looked forward to becoming grandparents, thinking it would be an event filled with joy and expectation. As it turned out, we lived through an agonizing year. Instead of the healthy baby girl we eagerly awaited, doctors discovered that our first grandchild would be born with defective kidneys, an enlarged heart and liver, and a virus infecting her intestines.

There was the suggestion of abortion, which the parents would not consider. So Mary Elizabeth was brought into this world a month early by cesarean section. She weighed one pound, fourteen ounces, and the doctors looked grim.

The first time we saw our tiny miracle, she had tubes coming out all over her body. We couldn't break down though because the parents were in desperate need of support. We had to be strong for them. We took turns giving twenty-four-hour care after Mary Elizabeth was allowed to go home. She went back to the hospital many times during her first year, back to the tubes and monitors, and all we could do was pray and try to get some rest. We never prayed so hard in our entire lives. A nationwide prayer chain of believers prayed faithfully for our Mary Elizabeth.

At four months, her heart was pronounced OK. Shortly after that, the liver improved dramatically, the intestinal virus went away, and then came the unforgettable day last fall when the doctors said she would make it. Even the worrisome kidneys had matured and were now draining properly.

Today, at sixteen months, our precious granddaughter is doing just fine, learning new words every day, and bringing great joy to our whole family.

I hope you will print this letter to encourage other grandparents whose grandchildren get a rocky start in life but find that God is faithful. He answers prayer and is still performing miracles.

A.   Thank you for your inspiring letter. Many grandparents and parents alike who are in prayer for newborns in crisis do not have such positive results. They pray and hope and trust and accept. Miracles, large and small, come from God. He formed the baby in the womb, guided the hands of the surgeons and nurses. He answered prayer in His way and in His time. The Holy Spirit flowed through praying friends.

God loves Mary Elizabeth. Let me challenge you to spend the rest of your life teaching your granddaughter to love God. Now that she is learning to talk, teach her words like *surrender, commitment,* and *unconditional love* so that, as she grows, her Christian walk will be another miracle that impacts others for Christ.

> God also testified to it by signs, wonders and various miracles, and gifts of the Holy Spirit distributed according to his will.
>
> Hebrews 2:4

The Special Needs Grandchild

Q. I looked forward to my first grandchild when I was forty-four. I prepared. I expected a normal grandchild. That's what healthy daughters are supposed to give you.

The doctor's words stung: "missing chromosome," "delayed development." I was sick, sick for all of us.

For a long time, I resented the active, adorable children I saw everywhere I went. I winced at baby magazines and children on TV ads. I prayed a lot, and one day, many months later, I knew I couldn't go on this way. I had to face the truth. I began volunteering in a special needs classroom, feeding children, wiping faces, and diapering bottoms. I heard a phrase there: "See the child, not the disability." I began to look at my granddaughter differently.

My daughter accepted everything all along. I am so proud of her. I'm a better grandparent now. I don't know if I qualify as "normal," but I do know I adore my grandchild, and she loves me just the way I am.

A. Thank you for your letter. Just as for a parent, the news that a grandchild has been born "different" is a shock that feels, as one grandmother put it, "like someone has piled up all of your hopes and dreams and smashed them to bits."

There's a beautiful Scripture verse in 1 Corinthians 15 that will quiet our fear for a newborn with disabilities. Paul is speaking of heavenly bodies, but his words also offer a clear explanation of how God values each and every child. Meditate on verse 41 as you pray for your disabled and very special grandchild: "The sun has one kind of splendor, the moon another and the stars another; and star differs from star in splendor" (1 Cor. 15:41).

God bless your splendid little star, and God bless all of you grandparents who are standing with parents of special needs children.

Every child is unique before God.

GRANDMOTHER, GRANDFATHER

Grandparenting Together

Q. I am a grandfather who is tired of having to go along with my wife's ideas when it comes to our grandson. He's eight years old, and he's real smart. He's my buddy, and we have fun together until Grandma steps in with her "Pick that up," "Do it this way," or "Here, I'll do it and get it done right."

The only peace we get is out fishing on the lake close by. How can I get her to understand that my grandson and I need time together and don't need to be regulated so much?

A. I wonder if you've told your wife how you feel. It sounds like she feels a little left out of your relationship with your grandson. I'm sure you don't mean to do that, but straight talk delivered with love is sorely missing in some families today.

Be sure you are expressing your feelings to your wife in a loving way, and receive her comments the same way. Be prepared to listen. Your wife may come up with things you would not think of. It will help if you make time for her to participate in some of your activities together. Then your time alone with your grandson won't be quite so threatening to her.

Enlist the help of your grandson's parents. They must know how much you and your grandson mean to each other. Let them be your allies in keeping the peace.

Try arranging to pick up your grandson for outings when your wife is otherwise occupied. Choose your visits carefully to avoid hurt feelings.

Remember, Grandma loves him too. She may have different ways of showing that, and different isn't necessarily wrong. Communicating a compromise will keep your differences working together for the sake of your grandson.

Husband and wife
should not lay down their heads at night
with a problem between them.

Ephesians 4:26, *paraphrased*

The Artificial Grandfather

Q. My husband goes with me to see the grandchildren, but he usually stands on one foot, then the other, wishing he were somewhere else. When the kids come over to our house, he reads his paper and basically acts like a nonentity over in the corner. He looks like a grandfather, but he's like an artificial Christmas tree. He's not real with the kids, and they know it. I've talked to him about this, and he replies that he isn't needed, that their grandmother can handle everything, so he just stays out of the way. How can I get him to change, or is it hopeless?

A. Telling you that he is not needed by his grandchildren could be a cop-out, or it could stem from low self-esteem that goes perhaps as far back as his own childhood and his parenting and grandparenting models. While there is no guarantee he will ever become a demonstrative, loving grandfather, there are a few things you might try.

First, get him to talk about his childhood, reflect on his grandparents and parents. My guess is that he had few, if any, loving seniors in his early life. Ask him how that felt. Praise him for who he is and for his accomplishments so that he feels safe to open up a little more. Then, arrange for him to be alone with the children. Capable, clever, caring grandmothers can unknowingly take center stage in a grandchild's life, leaving grandfather behind the curtain. With the parents' permission, make dates for grandfather to drive the children to a favorite place where they can spend a few hours together, alone. When the children come to your house, occasionally take a trip to the market, leaving them and grandfather together to fend for themselves.

Your husband needs to know he is needed, and we all know how much the children need him! Here are only a few needs a child has that a grandfather can fill.

- To develop a sense of belonging and acceptance
- To learn skills that make life interesting and values that are essential to healthy physical and spiritual growth
- To experience fun and fantasy
- To be encouraged to explore the untried
- To make good memories
- To have an understanding and nonjudgmental listener and potential source of advice

Collaborate with your children to help your husband reach out and grab his rightful place in his grandchildren's lives. One day he will thank you for it.

Grandparenting as a Second Job

Q. Both my husband and I still work and will for another five years or so. We don't have much time for our grandchildren, who are three and six. We do our best, but we don't ever want to be known as letting our children down. We love our grandchildren dearly and want to be normal grandparents.

A. Good grandparenting should be looked upon as a full-time ministry, not an obligation or an assignment. Stay active in the lives of your two grandchildren by building your grandparenting around your jobs.

Think of it as your second job. Make time for outings. Pick up the telephone. Write that note of encouragement, and drop it in the mail or stop by after work.

I received a letter from a grandmother who works in real estate and is on call seven days a week. As often as she can, she leaves the office before four o'clock and drops by to spend a few minutes with her toddler granddaughter. They have a tea party together in the girl's room. It only takes a half hour, and it is the stuff of which memories are made—for both of them.

A letter from another grandmother said, "For years my granddaughter and I would have make-believe tea parties in her room. Now that she is older, she doesn't take me by the hand down the hall to her room anymore. I miss that dreadfully, but at least I can relive the memories."

In the blink of an eye, they will be grown up. Treasure the moments. Better than a paycheck, you can live the rest of your life on the rewards of a faithful grandparenting ministry.

The Importance of Planning

Q. I need help right away. Our fourteen-year-old granddaughter arrives in thirty days to stay the summer with us while her folks are on a mission to Mexico. We had her last year, too, and things did not go well between my husband and me. We argued a lot privately about how to treat our granddaughter's schedule, keeping her occupied, and allowing her certain freedoms while she was here. I think we need to know where she is at all times for safety reasons. My husband thinks we should give the girl more time on her own at age fourteen.

Please advise us before she comes. I don't think I can make it through another summer like the last one.

A. Your important first step is to make a plan that you and your husband can agree on, and then stick to it. Do it *now*. Think ahead about possible scenarios during the coming summer, and prepare for all eventualities.

Tear three months out of a calendar and tape them to your refrigerator, mapping out events, big and small. In the squares where nothing is planned, mark it "hugs." Remember, girls her age like to have time to themselves, so don't overplan. Careful, thoughtful planning brings balance and peace of mind because everyone knows what will happen. You both have to give in a little, but you'll gain more than you lose.

Contact your grandchild's parents for ideas and advice. Tell them you want this to be an especially meaningful time for your granddaughter. There will have been a number of changes in her life in the past year. Learn what those are, and plan accordingly. Fourteen can be a tough age for some girls. Boys, music, noise, and friends top their list.

Be sure to make an agreement with your granddaughter's parents on issues such as nighttime curfew, telephone use, spending money, treats, and TV viewing. Then, if there is rebellion, you can remind your granddaughter that you are following orders from her parents.

If both of you keep a happy attitude, keep communicating with each other, and work together, you'll be fine. Have a great summer!

Widowhood Changes Everything

Q. I'm a newly widowed seventy-one-year-old grandmother of seven with two great-grandchildren. We are a large, loving Christian family, all living close by. Things have changed, though, because my husband was the children's favorite, and he's gone now. I don't feel quite so much a part of the young families' lives these days. I don't guess there's much I can do about it.

A. Whether you become single by death or divorce, there is one thing you can count on: things will change. Attitudes, friends or those you thought were friends, even family members, will change. When death occurs and grief takes over, it can be hard to remember that everyone in the family has experienced the great loss along with you. Your pain feels deeper because he was your life partner, but your children and others who knew your husband well are also grieving in their own way.

I don't know how recently you became a widow, but I urge you to try to avoid the loneliness of personal grief by filling your own life with worthwhile projects and people. That's probably what your dear husband would have wanted you to do. Go on. Make a difference.

If funds allow, travel. Take a good friend with you. Take a grandchild or great-grandchild with you. Join a philanthropic organization that works for the good of the community. Be more active in your church; there are never enough willing hands there. Fill your days and nights with good choices, happy occasions, and friends who understand.

As a Christian, you know that your life is not in a child, a grandchild, or even a friend. Your life is in Jesus Christ. He is the One who validates your existence. It is not how you are received by family that gives your life purpose and meaning, but what Christ has done for you by His death on the Cross.

Do not fall prey to self-pity or resentment. Begin today a new life. You will rejoice in the reaction of your family to the example you set.

"NORMAL" GRANDPARENTING

What Is Normal Anyway?

Q. We're delighted to be the brand-new grandparents of a bouncing baby boy. Friends have given us a lot of ideas and advice on grandparenting, so much that I am confused by conflicting opinions. Is there such a thing as "normal" grandparenting?

A. What is normal for one may not be normal for another. Some families build expectations based on previous generations. Children's expectations may be high if there has been a long history of exemplary grandparents. Those who had negative or no role models for grandparenting might do the wrong things while trying to do the right things, or they might even force their style on others.

The only way to succeed as a grandparent is to be your wonderful self, follow biblical guidelines, and be available when the young family has needs of any kind. Then be the kind of grandparent that your family members know instinctively they can come to in times of trouble or sorrow. Bring them joy and happiness by unexpected touches of kindness. Teach them from your own life experiences, good and bad. And when you fall down, either from your own lofty ambitions or their unreasonable expectations, pick yourself up, dust yourself off with forgiveness, and start again.

I Don't Want to Be Normal!

Q. My parents tell me I was not a normal kid. Not that I was weird or anything—I just did my own thing in my own style. My husband and I have a very happy marriage because we do the unexpected for each other. We have two happy grown-up kids we are crazy about.

Surprises are fun, and life is too short to try to fit it into someone else's idea of what is OK or normal. Now, we're about to be grandparents and, by cracky, we don't plan to be stereotypical grandparents either! Do you see anything wrong with that?

A. No! We all have the freedom to grandparent with our own special style. As a child, my friend Rose regularly received penny checks from her grandfather, one cent to be spent anyway she liked. Today, she gleefully watches her own daughter receive those checks from her great-grandfather.

Another friend remembers feeling safe in the red car seat with the steering wheel that his grandparents bought for him to play with when he rode in their car. Today, the red car seat with the steering wheel remains in Grandfather's car, even though the child has long since become a man.

Betty and Jack were expectant grandparents who stayed with the other set of expectant grandparents all night at the hospital, waiting for a first glimpse at their first grandchild. After the blessed event finally happened, the weary seniors exchanged high fives and congratulated each other on the good job they had done, to the delight of the new parents and the hospital staff.

Make your own special mark. They'll probably be talking about you two for generations to come and with a big smile!

We never outgrow
our need to be appreciated.[6]

GRANDPARENTING BY GOD'S GRACE

Passing on Your Values

Q. I had no grandparenting models when I was growing up, and my husband's grandparents were quite old and cranky before they passed away. We want to begin a new era of good grandparenting for our grandchildren. We have three, all close by. We do our best to give them quality time when we're together; we plan things and make special efforts. I don't spoil them, but they know I love them. There have been few discipline problems, mainly because of the excellent Christian training they get at home. We are just enjoying our grandchildren tremendously but would appreciate any ideas on how we can show them how we live and all that they can look forward to in their own lives. We wouldn't *ever* want to cause them to stumble.

A. You've asked a very important question, and it shows just how seriously you take this job. Congratulations.

Let your precious ones see these truths by the way you live and who you are:

- That you love God and know that He loves you
- That you are honest, consistent, and trustworthy
- That you never knowingly hurt anyone by thought or action
- That you have been rewarded for hard work
- That you love your country
- That you always have time to listen to them

- That you love them, even when they make mistakes
- That you are tolerant of all races and creeds
- That you find the joy in every circumstance
- That you will not compromise your faith

Grandparenting by Grace

Q. Please explain what you mean by "grandparenting by God's grace."

A. It is by God's free gift of grace that we have this job, and it is by His grace that we live it every day. Understanding these truths helps a grandparent to find the joy in every circumstance and to have victory over the trials, knowing that God's grace is sufficient.

The essence of grandparenting by God's grace is love. A grandparent who has lived a life riddled with mistakes can know that there is still some of God's love in him or her, however damaged that life may be. That love can be passed on to a grandchild. It is a gift from God that enables and empowers grandparents to be the best they can be, to enjoy their role in the family, and to make a difference by their love.

Grandparenting by grace is more than telling the gospel truths. It is living them.

> I do not account my life of any value nor as precious to myself, if only I may accomplish my course and the ministry which I received from the Lord Jesus, to testify to the gospel of the grace of God.
>
> Acts 20:24, RSV

> Let us then approach the throne of grace with confidence, so that we may receive mercy and find grace to help us in our time of need.
>
> Hebrews 4:16

The Basics of Good Grandparenting

HAVING A SENSE OF HUMOR

LEAVING A LEGACY

The Basics of Good Grandparenting

A GOOD GRANDPARENT WILL	A GOOD GRANDPARENT WILL NOT
• Partner in planning	• Meddle
• Counsel when asked	• Spoil
• Advise when consulted	• Discourage
• Listen	• Usurp parental authority
• Keep confidences	• Show favoritism
• Encourage	• Be absent
• Pray	• Criticize
• Baby-sit when available	• Overindulge
• Have fun	• Oversymphathize
• Model Christ	• Ever run out of love

Most of us have a natural desire or drive to grandparent. We look forward to it. We may go into the job emulating excellent role models from our own growing up, or we may carry old baggage from negative or absent models.

Deep down, though, every grandparent wants to be good at it. You may be anticipating the event, or perhaps you've just claimed the title—again. Section 2 answers critical questions about the basics of grandparenting. You'll see that a good grandparent has a good attitude, maturity, a good memory, and a sense of humor. A good grandparent is courageous, flexible, has staying power, and, above all, is loving. Love is the basis for everything a good grandparent does and says.

There's no need for good looks or a good bank balance. The greatest quality of a good grandparent is love.

> So faith, hope, love abide, these three;
> but the greatest of these is love.
> 1 Corinthians 13:13, RSV

WHO'S IN CHARGE?

Offering Your Opinion

Q. Is it appropriate for grandparents to tell parents when a child needs professional help? We are in our late fifties and travel sixty miles regularly to see our son and daughter-in-law's family. During our visits, we have noticed a consistent pattern of mood swings on the part of our six-year-old granddaughter, our only grandchild. She is an intelligent girl, gets good marks at school, and has many friends, but there's a melancholy about her. She withdraws and pouts for no apparent reason. She greets us warmly, then, after we've been there a few minutes, she refuses to even talk to us. Her mother sends her to her room.

We wonder, is it us? We show her only love and have a good relationship with her parents. I think our granddaughter needs professional help. I don't want to risk alienating her parents but I'm feeling a need to tell them.

A. Your question "Is it us?" requires an answer. Rather than barging in with advice, try asking the parents this question: "Does Susie withdraw from others or only when her grandfather and I come over?"

They may have known the answer to this difficult question for some time but have not known how to tell you. For example, your cologne or makeup may be offensive to your little granddaughter. Perhaps she feels bombarded by questions and hugs, or something her grandfather says or does makes her shy away. If this is indeed the problem, a few explanations by the parents to the child will make your granddaughter feel better, more relaxed, and responsive to you.

Then again, the answer to your brave question may have nothing to do with you. The parents might be glad someone else has noticed their daughter's odd behavior and frustrated that trying to change it by sending her to her room isn't working. A physical exam will rule out allergies or any deficiency in her system that could cause personality changes or mood swings.

You will enjoy a more open working relationship with the parents simply by asking such an up-front question, "Is it us?" You also will enhance your opportunities to be an influence in your granddaughter's life as she grows older and needs your wisdom.

Get your courage up and ask. It's the loving thing to do.

Discipline at Your House

Q. What should I do when there doesn't seem to be any discipline at my grandchildren's house, and then they come over to see us and think they can get away with murder? The last time was the last straw! At ages ten and thirteen, our grandsons should know better than to get into their grandfather's tools. We tell them to keep out of the garage, but they go right in. They have no fear. I could give you many other examples of outright disobedience.

I had a talk with their mother, who said she would talk with the kids. That was some time ago, but there has been no improvement. They're over often, so I would appreciate your advice.

A. Lack of parental discipline can raise your blood pressure and your doctor bills! Before another situation arises, have one more conversation with *both* parents. Ask them what they want you to do or say when the children get into dangerous tools or when they won't mind. Could it be that the parents do not know the extent of the boys' misbehavior?

The general rule for grandparents who see a need for more discipline in their grandchildren is to find out what happens at home so they can reinforce the same discipline when the children come to their house. Often you have to ask to find out. Does Mom give time-outs? Does the child get sent to his room? Is a disciplinary swat allowed? Some parents assume that the grandparents know more than they actually know about the discipline methods they've chosen for their children.

When there's no at-home discipline at all, however, another approach is called for. Confront the parents (not the children)—with love.

Poor Approach:	"You'd better put a little discipline in these children's lives before it's too late, because if you don't, there's going to be trouble!"
Better Approach:	"I'm concerned, dear. I want to do the right thing, and I need your help when it comes to disciplining the kids when they're over."

Notice the difference between using accusatory *you* statements versus the heartfelt, loving concern in the *I* statements. If you think such a conversation is out of the question or your loving words have already fallen on deaf ears, you can at least take the following measures:

- Report to the parent any verbal, emotional, or physical abuse from a grandchild.
- Do not excuse property damage. Report it, and love the child from a distance until the behavior is gone.
- Do not ignore self-destructive habits such as drug abuse. You can try to talk with your grandchild, but the parent has ultimate responsibility for discipline, especially in such serious matters.
- Use tough love principles. "We don't do that here! Would you rather just go home now, and we'll talk with your parent(s)?"

"I'll wait one minute for the real (child's name) to return. If he doesn't, this one will be sent to bed!"

- Physical punishment for disobedience in your home is taboo unless you have approval and understanding from the parents. The risks are just too great. Parents are the gatekeepers to your relationship with your grandchildren. Clear communication will keep the gate open.

Manners

Q. Our grandchildren are a joy to us. We have a girl who is six and a boy who is ten. We have wonderful times together, and we have lots of love and respect for the parents. There's just one thing.

Our grandchildren's manners are atrocious!

No "thank-yous." No "Please, may I . . . ." Food is eaten noisily, and they're off without asking to be excused. They yell at each other rather than asking for something in a normal tone of voice. They don't ask. They give orders!

They rip open gifts. They don't knock before they enter a closed door. I could go on, but you get the picture.

I know their family life is fast-paced, with both parents working and a busy schedule at home, school, and church. Am I expecting too much?

A. You are expecting too much from the children but not from their parents, who should be as aware of these bad manners as you are. Try mentioning it casually to your child. Don't make a big deal about it. Recall for him the manners training you gave him when he was little and how proud you were of the many courtesies he displayed as he grew up. Let him know he is doing a good job in a fast-paced life and you'd like to help.

Remember that you have opportunities to teach your grandchildren every time you are around them. There's little you can do about what happens at their home. When the children are at *your* house, though, teach them *your* manners. For instance,

- Explain mealtime manners: Don't begin to eat until after the blessing. Use a napkin. Say "please pass . . ." and "thank-you."
- Congratulate them when they do it right.
- Ask your ten-year-old grandson to open the door for his little sister and you. Praise and thank him profusely for doing it. Soon he'll do it without prompting.
- Use a moderate tone of voice, even when it's hard to do.
- When introducing a friend your age to the children, teach them to stand as they greet the guest.
- Ask your grandchildren to help you. Don't order them.
- Stop them when they run in your house. Detain them with conversation and ask if they have forgotten something (such as an apology).
- Always knock on their doors.
- Weave good manners into the stories you tell in quiet times.
- Always show your grandchildren kindness and gentleness.[1]

Yes, these are things they should be learning at home, but you can't teach there. Your house, however, is a perfectly legitimate teaching field. Take advantage of every opportunity to model for them what you teach. June Hines Moore's book *You Can Raise a Well-Mannered Child* is an excellent resource for teaching manners.

Different Parenting Styles

Q. Sometimes it's all I can do to keep still about what I see and hear regarding the discipline of my grandchildren. One of our daughters has this idea that the boys, ages eleven and eight, can do anything they please as long as they don't hurt anybody or anything. She says they have been taught the difference between right and wrong and need to learn from their own mistakes. This results in near chaos when these two children are in our house at the same time as our other two grandchildren, who are almost the same age.

Our son's two boys are well behaved, even shy. They have strict rules of conduct at home, reinforced by our daughter-in-law. Both of these little boys are well loved, well adjusted, happy children, don't mistake me. They just know how to act and are pleasant to be around. The other two are boisterous and spoiled, taunting and causing trouble for the others. What can I do?

A. *Can* is the operative word here. What you *can't* do is tell your children how to raise their children. You know that when they married and formed their own family unit, you lost whatever control you had over them.

What you *can* do is tell your daughter the truth about what goes on when the four children are together. If she doesn't get the message, stop inviting her children over, especially when their cousins are to be there. Do not point out the differences between her parenting style and that of her sister-in-law, or you'll create ill will between them. Stick to the facts of the behavior of her two children, and let her know that it is stressful for you and that you would appreciate anything she can do to resolve it.

If it doesn't get resolved, visit her family at *her* house only. Unlike your home, you can always walk out when the going gets rough.

> In order to discipline a grandchild,
> we must know what happens at their house.

Following the Rules at Mealtime

Q. My daughter-in-law and I get along pretty well except when it comes to what the kids eat when they are at our house. She has a strict diet for them with no fat, no sugar, etc., and insists they stick to it even when they're with us. I don't think a little treat hurts anything once in a while, and this is, after all, *my* house. I set the rules. Please answer before a perfectly good relationship goes down the drain.

A. You have a right to set the rules in your house for whomever lives in your house. Short-term visitors and guests are another matter. In the case of your grandchildren, rules have already been set in *their* house. Mom has a right to ask that those rules be kept when the kids are guests in your home.

Exceptions are in their behavior. You don't want to let a child run rampant in your house or assault you with bad language. But when it comes to what you put in their tummies, Mom's the boss, not Grandma.

SETTING BOUNDARIES

Baby-Sitting

Q. My daughter thinks I don't have a life of my own. I give up going and doing to baby-sit my grandchildren. I want to help her out, but it's getting to be too much, and I'm not getting any younger. How can I let her know about this without causing a problem between us?

A. You are being "dumped on." Your situation cries for boundaries! You can still lay them down, with love. Every grandparent wants to see those babies and to help Mom out, but we shouldn't have to suffer for it. Here are rules of thumb if you are going to continue to supply this free service that's costing you plenty:

- Before the next baby-sitting assignment, set a time and place to talk to your daughter about what's going on in *your* life. Tell her the good things you are doing and what's ahead for you. Tell her how much you love to baby-sit the children and the joy it brings you as you watch them grow. Let her know gently that you need more time for yourself and your goals. Then give her a schedule of your availability, days and times. A caring parent will understand and mend her ways.
- Request a twenty-four-hour notice when your services are needed.
- Have the courage to say no if you have plans.

Spoiling

Q. Our kids think I spoil my granddaughter. I really don't. I just love her. I loved her before she was born. She is ten months old now and a darling baby. I buy her things, and when I go to see her, she squeals with glee. When I arrive, she crawls right over and wants to sit on my lap. My daughter feels that I should not buy her presents except on birthdays and such and that I am too extravagant. I buy her clothes and toys, which I can afford.

I have three grown children: two sons, ages nineteen and twenty-one, who are unmarried and my married daughter, who is twenty-four. I raised them with love and common sense, and they are all very nice kids.

Am I spoiling my granddaughter by loving her?

A. Of course you're not spoiling your granddaughter by loving her. Grandparent love and attention helps to lay a foundation of trust and security for the baby in that first year of life.

The *way* you show that deep love, however, might spoil your relationship with your daughter. Put yourself in her place. I assume she's a first-time mom. For the past ten months, she's been learning that job by trial and error. Surely she is aware that you are far more experienced and far better equipped financially to provide for her baby. The only thing she felt sure about was the love of her baby, and now she's afraid her baby might like you better. The way you are loving your grandchild is intimidating to your daughter.

Back off a little with the presents. Abide by the parents' wishes on extravagant gifts. Show honor and respect to your daughter by picking up your granddaughter, hugging her, then handing her to her mother. You'll get your share of cuddling time, but you won't be monopolizing the baby.

When you have so much love to give, it's hard to play second fiddle, but that's just what you are. Mom is Mom, and that means she comes first, and rightly so.

Think about this as well: When grandparent gift giving is extravagant, what expectations are you creating in the child as she grows older?

Taking Over

Q. I baby-sit my sixteen-month-old grandson five days a week while my daughter-in-law works. I do it for nothing to help out, but lately my daughter-in-law has been accusing me of mothering her son because he has a tantrum when she picks him up to go home. I know my place. I love and care for him, and we play a lot. I told her it's natural for him to want to stay where he has fun all day and that he'll get over it. What do you suggest I do about this situation? It's getting pretty hostile.

A. It sounds like you might have overstepped your boundaries, Grandma, undoubtedly out of love for your grandchild. It's easy to blur that fine line between baby-sitting as a grandmother and becoming a second mother to the child. You have crossed that line, at least from your daughter-in-law's perspective.

It really isn't natural for your grandson to want to stay where he has fun all day. Children need structure, discipline, and goals just as much as they need to be entertained.

Strike a balance in your daily care by including some ways to keep the mother a vital part of the child's day, even though she is absent. Make handmade gifts the child can present to her when she arrives to take him home. Talk about Mother in loving ways, so your grandson will look forward to her coming. You probably won't have to say a word to your daughter-in-law. The changes she'll see in her child will speak volumes.

One of the hardest things for a loving grandparent to accept is who's in charge. You are the daily caregiver five times a week. Mom is the primary caregiver seven days a week. It's up to you as a grandparent to love your grandson enough to nurture his relationship with his mother.

Bragging

Q. I have the world's greatest grandkids! Both of them, a boy, twelve, and a girl, fifteen, are so gorgeous and smart. Ever since they were born, I have wanted to get up on the roof and shout to the whole world just how terrific they are. I carry a brag book on each one and show it to anyone who'll look. I have all of their annual school pictures in it.

And I love to tell them that I love them. I tell them they are beautiful and the best and that God loves them. I know some people think I overdo it, but I don't care. What do you think of bragging about grandchildren?

A. I wouldn't qualify what you have described as bragging. It's more like unconditional love, and I think it's great! At twelve and fifteen, your grandchildren's self-esteem is fragile. I'm glad they have you in their corner, encouraging and building them up to counteract the inevitable self-doubt and negativity that will creep into their young lives.

Bragging is an overstatement of the truth. Even though kids love to hear it, they know when we have overstepped the boundaries of truth. In some cases, we need to acknowledge that bragging can be embarrassing.

I prefer the term *honoring* because it implies that the child is being noticed for something he really did and as someone he really is. A good example of this is a grandfather in the Northwest who takes every opportunity to show his love and pride in his grandson. One way is by introducing him to friends, not as "John, my grandson," but as "John, my grandson who is captain of the basketball team."

Another grandfather surprises his granddaughter when friends are over by asking her to share with them what is happening in her life at school and at church. There are many ways to "brag" about grandchildren by honoring not only their achievements but the fact that they are alive and they belong to you!

Keep it up, Grandma! You remind me of a little fellow I met in an elementary classroom when I asked the students, "How do you know your grandma really loves you?" His face lit up as he responded, "Because when I look in her eyes, I can see all the way to her heart! She's nuts about me!"

GIFT GIVING

Giving Appropriate Gifts

Q. My daughter and her family live in another state, and I am just about ready to quit giving my grandchildren gifts altogether! All I get back is ingratitude. I heard recently that one gift I sent my nine-year-old grandson was thrown on the floor as soon as it was opened. It was a baseball mitt, a good one. He said he hated baseball and wouldn't have a thing to do with the new mitt. What do you make of that?

A. Your generous heart has been in the right place, but you are not aware of the interests of at least one of your grandchildren. To be effective gift givers, we need to know what activities and special interests our grandchildren have. That is more difficult when they live far away but nonetheless important.

Next time birthdays roll around, write or telephone the parents, and ask some questions in advance. Better yet, talk with your grandchild by phone, showing that you are interested in the things that occupy his thoughts and time. That way, you can choose an appropriate gift that will be welcomed.

Sometimes it feels like grandchildren are pretty insensitive about what we try to do for them. When we look beneath the surface, however, we usually find an underlying reason of misunderstanding or a lack of communication. It's not a fault on your part, just a signal that perhaps you need to be in closer touch with your long-distance loved ones.

Grandchild Gifts under Five Dollars

Q. Everything is so expensive today. I have to spend an arm and a leg to buy a gift for my grandchildren. Do you know some things I can get for five dollars or less? I have seventeen grandchildren.

A.   Believe it or not, there are some things you can buy your grandchild for five dollars or less. I have two lists for you to consider:

List 1:   *Gifts that cost five dollars or less:*
Two video rentals, two bags of miniature candy bars, tennis balls, a baseball, a child's soccer ball, ten pounds of unpopped popcorn, car wax, two coupons for fast-food meals, a ticket to a minor league game, a coloring book and crayons, stamps, twenty-five postcards, a gift certificate, cologne, socks, a living plant, bubble bath, a small stuffed animal, a scrapbook, bookmarks, a children's Bible, and books, books, books.

List 2:   *Gifts that cost nothing:*
One handwritten certificate for one trip to the zoo or one favorite homemade cake or pie or one special dinner at your house, one freshly cut bouquet of flowers from your yard, or one Saturday afternoon in Grandpa's workshop.

Then there are the gifts of eternal value: your Christian faith, encouragement, a listening ear, a soft shoulder, friendship, and a hunger for God's Word. These are free gifts. Without them, however, a grandchild might learn the most expensive lessons of a lifetime.

The most valuable gifts grandparents can give grandchildren are themselves.

Yesterday is gone, tomorrow is yet to be.
Today is called the "present." That makes it a gift.

Responding to Needs

A House of Their Own

Q.   Our two grandchildren live in a cramped apartment with our son and his wife. They don't have much money, and we'd like to help them get into a house. We're not rich, either, so we'd appreciate any thoughts before we go ahead. These kids work hard and deserve a home.

A. For the sake of our grandchildren, we grandparents want to do what we can for our grown children. Some react rather than thoughtfully respond. You are wise to pause and ask some questions.

If you personally loan the money for the house, make a written plan. Planning brings balance and responsibility and sets a good example. Clearly communicate your intentions and expectations in all financial transactions, even at the risk of temporarily jeopardizing your relationship with your child. And if a grandchild ever asks for a loan, make sure you consult with the parents before you agree, or you'll risk your relationship with them for sure!

Stick to the plan. Don't cave in on late payments. Keep your child responsible for what he owes you, even if it hurts.

Did you know that you don't have to be the source of funds when your children have needs? Instead, you can be part of the process to answering that need. Visit a financial planner for new, innovative ideas on helping children acquire their first home. There are ways to satisfy that need while allowing your children to maintain their independence and you to keep your net worth. There are even some tax and investment benefits in shared ownership, for example. Check it out. Financial partnering is a tangible way to say, "I trust you. I believe in you." Consider matching funds. The kids come up with a certain amount; you match it in the form of a loan.

There are many helpful books on the market dealing with giving and loaning money to children. Authors Larry Burkett, Ron Blue, and Judith Briles are good sources.

Rules for Giving and Loaning Money

Q. My husband and I have had a visit from our daughter and son-in-law. They made kind of a formal appointment with us to ask for a loan to buy a new car. We have had a few problems over their seven-year marriage, mostly in getting along with our son-in-law, who can't hold a job. We told them we'd get back with them about our decision. Should we give them the money?

A.   Only you can make this decision. If you do plan to give money, follow these rules:

- Don't give it if your motivation has anything to do with guilt about something that happened or didn't happen in the past.
- Don't give it if you are indulging them.
- Don't give it if you don't have it to give. Someday you may need it.
- Ask yourself whether this gift will make a positive or a negative influence on your child's incentive to make his or her own way in the world. Are you creating an expectation that money is always available?
- What are the tax implications of this gift or loan?

Keeping Adult Children Responsible

Q.   My husband and I have loaned money to our son and his wife on three occasions. Once we loaned $1,000 to pay overdue traffic tickets. Another time we paid off their Visa bill of $840 so they wouldn't lose the credit card. Then we loaned them $10,000 on a promissory note to get into their house. Last night, they came over asking for $3,000 more for furniture. My husband got pretty upset because the kids have defaulted so far on all three previous loans. He said no, and they left pretty hurt.

I agree with my husband on this, but it is very hard to say no when you know they have needs and there are three wonderful grandchildren involved. Now that we have said no, what should we do?

A.   Your first mistake was loaning money a second time without repayment of the first. Not only did your kids let you down, but you let them down by not holding their feet to the fire. You fostered their irresponsible behavior. The next mistake was the promissory note for the house. Even if the note spelled out a payment schedule, it was obviously ignored, and you allowed that to the extent that the kids felt they could come back to the money tree one more time.

Calm down and invite them over. Sit down together and make a payment schedule for all three loans. After three months of prompt payment on the amounts they owe you, you might add $3,000 to it. That is, if you can afford it. I don't know how old you are, but remember, there will come a time when you and your husband will need your money. Don't run yourself short.

Teach your grown child accountability and responsibility. Don't apologize for it. You've been most generous, and they have some making up to do.

When to Say No

Q. On days when I get to take my grandson to the mall for a few hours, he asks for quarters to play the video games. I give him three, then he wants three more, and then asks for even more. As he grows older, it gets harder to say no to his wants. His public whining is embarrassing. Some people look at me with sympathy, but some give me a look that makes me feel like some kind of ogre.

When should a grandparent say no when it comes to doling out small amounts of money to a grandchild?

A. By giving in every time, you are giving an inch, and your grandson is taking a mile. Try allowing video games every *other* time you go. Explain the number of quarters you are taking so the child understands that's all there is. Explain your plans for the trip. For example, "Today, we're going to see the children's petting zoo in the mall, and the next time, we'll play video games."

While you're at it, explain the very real fact that four quarters make one dollar, and you don't have a lot of them. Indiscriminate doling out devalues money in the child's eyes and creates the illusion that money is always there and that there is no need to work for it or be accountable for it. Help your grandson concentrate on the joy of being with you, the excitement of the trip. The whining will disappear as he grows with stronger, deeper values.

Keeping and Breaking Confidences

Q. Every other Saturday, my husband has a date with our eight- year-old granddaughter. At about eleven o'clock, they go to the lumberyard in town for supplies and then have a fast-food lunch and ice cream. The two of them are really close, so she feels extra safe talking to him about anything that's on her mind.

Lately, my husband has been puzzled by some comments our granddaughter has made. She seems to have lost her confidence, coming up with remarks like, "I'm not good enough" or "I can't win." She is a very bright, well-liked child in her neighborhood and at school. We wonder if she is under some extreme peer pressure from somewhere and whether we should tell her parents what we know.

A. Keeping confidences with grandchildren is paramount to a good relationship. Yet, your interest is in her welfare, all aspects of it. Don't rush to the phone or drive over to her parents, but the next time you are with them, try to find out what goes on in your granddaughter's life at school and at home. If you hear something that might be the root of your granddaughter's malaise, tell her parents that you've noticed her response to such a factor and offer suggestions as to a remedy. For example, the parent might say she has had a particularly hard time in a new school or making friends. Use that information to suggest more parental involvement so they can do the vital work of questioning their daughter, loving and understanding her, turning a negative into a positive.

Some grandparents make a mistake by running to the parents with every little thing they hear or perceive. When word gets back to the child, and it will, confidence may be destroyed, and a grandchild may not feel safe telling her grandparents anything.

Choose an appropriate time, and express your ideas to the parents in a concerned but loving way. Remember to bolster your granddaughter's self-esteem by telling her how beautiful, how smart, and how loved she is!

HAVING A SENSE OF HUMOR

Giving of Yourself Joyfully

Q. We were "grandparents in waiting" for ten years. Then came the baby boom! First a boy and then a girl were born to our oldest son. Then, twins came five years ago to our only daughter.

Now, our daughter is in her seventh month and has been ordered to strict bed rest for the remainder of this pregnancy. (She's only expecting one this time.) Of course, the twins are living with us until Mommy delivers. My husband and I have gone from doting grandparents to pseudo-parents of twins.

We are up at 6:30 A.M., dress, feed and clean up, take the twins to preschool, go back home, clean, wash, fold, change beds, prepare lunch, go back to preschool, bring the twins home, have lunch and naps (which is a joke), supervise playtime, think about dinner, make it, try to eat it, supervise playtime, give baths, and get ready for bedtime. Then we start again the next day. It's like déjà vu all over again. Been there. Done that.

We love our son-in-law. He works six days a week. This arrangement is really the best thing for everybody, and we asked for it.

I am a woman in control! I have been a corporate majordomo. I prepared for grandparenting by reading all the right books. I had it figured out and looked forward to it and enjoyed it—from a distance. Now I've got it up close and personal for the next two months. Any suggestions? Help!

A. You wrote it. I read it! "This arrangement is the best thing for everybody, and we asked for it." Bless your hearts; you'll make it.

Take pictures, tape videos. Keep a journal. Keep your wonderful sense of humor. You will all look back on this time with a lot of laughs and indescribable love and gratitude. Yes, I said *gratitude.* The earthquake you feel is the rumble of good works.

Attack every day as a new day. Soon it will be over, and, crazy as it may seem, you'll wish you could do it again.

My answer is probably not what you wanted to hear, but, you're a blessed grandparent to be trusted with your grandtwins. You've proved yourself time and time again through your career, your marriage, your parenting, and now you have an opportunity to do it again as a grandparent.

And who are you really doing it for? That precious one who will be born in two months. What stories you will have to tell!

The Blessings of a Merry Heart

Q. I confess. I backed my car out of my son-in-law's driveway into his garbage can. I totaled the poor thing (the can, that is). My daughter was horrified because she's married to a neat freak—you know, everything in its place. So before he could find out about it, I went to the store and bought him a new garbage can, then filled it with freshly popped popcorn. I swore my grandson to secrecy. He told me that when his dad got home, he thought the garbage can was a different color, went over to it, lifted the lid, and laughed his head off, saying, "Your grandmother's been here!"

It didn't hurt so much when he got the full story, and we're still friends. You might say I have a reputation in the family for keeping things light—Like the time my grandson's rabbit ran off, and I bought him a new one. She was pregnant, and very soon there were nine cute little bunnies in the hutch. My son-in-law liked that a lot.

A.   Thanks for your great letter. We can all use a dose of good humor today. I have a hunch your entire family thanks God for you and your individuality, even your son-in-law.

I hope you never lose your sense of humor. A measure of our maturity as grandparents is the ability to see the joy and fun in any circumstance. Without it, the inevitable bumps in the road of life become mountains we never get over.

A merry heart is like medicine.
Keep your family healthy!

Finding Joy When Life Is Joyless

Q.   I find in recent years that it is harder and harder to be happy. In public, people are so rude. The world seems full of takers. There's so much crime in our neighborhood that my husband and I are afraid to go out after six. We are in our late sixties and have raised four children, all of whom live in other states because of their jobs. That makes us long-distance grandparents on a fixed income, and we miss out on the joy of being with our family. They visit rarely because they are busy.

It just feels like the joy has gone out of life for us. We watch TV, go to the store, and that's about all.

A.   I was saddened by your letter, so let's see if we can't change your circumstances.

First of all, there will always be rude people and takers. We have to ignore them and try not to put ourselves in their company.

Second, is there any chance you can move to another neighborhood? I know moving sounds like a daunting task, but it might be worth investigating. Ask one of those busy children of yours to assist you in a search for a safer neighborhood, perhaps nearer to them.

Then, about those grandchildren. There are many things you can do to keep that important link, things that don't cost a lot. The "Long-

Distance Grandparenting" part of section 6 of *Grandparenting: It's Not What It Used To Be* will give you some ideas for turning a new leaf of correspondence and contact with your family. It's important, and you will reap great rewards.

Now, I have a personal question for you. How long has it been since you and your husband had a complete physical exam? You could be experiencing a minor deficiency in your systems that could be easily restored, giving you more energy and a new outlook.

Lastly, let me encourage you to concentrate on the positives in your life. You have your health, your mobility, your home, your children and grandchildren, and many more years ahead of you. Make those years count, remembering that they are a gift from the Lord, who loves you and wants you to be happy.

> Happy is he who trusts in the Lord.
> Proverbs 16:20b, RSV

LEAVING A LEGACY

Temporary Versus Eternal Gifts

Q. My husband and I have been entrusted with a good amount of the Lord's money. We earned it as longtime schoolteachers and college professors. We are faithful tithers, helped build the new sanctuary, and support foreign and home missions projects.

We have also put three of our children through college and two grandchildren through a private university. Our family members have always counted on us to help in major ways, and we have never let them down.

Now we are coming to old age and are wondering about how to pass on some of the money to our grandchildren. Would you suggest that we do that while we are still alive or put it in a trust fund to be initiated after we pass on?

A. It depends on a number of factors: the needs of the children, their hopes and dreams as expressed to you, and their abilities to achieve those hopes and dreams. It depends on what you envision lies ahead in the life of each child and how best to impact that life for good. Do you want to see the children prosper while you are still alive? Do you want to receive their gratitude and see the joy and progress you have provided by your gift? Or do those things not matter to you, and you would prefer to surprise them?

These choices are individual and personal. Money poured into bricks and mortar is not nearly as valuable as the love, truth, and joy of knowing the risen Lord that has been poured into your grandchildren by your example. Christlike modeling and teaching about God every day of your life is an eternal legacy of far greater value to your grandchildren, and it's never too late to start as long as God gives you life and breath.

Give them your money in the way that is right for them and for you, but make sure that your final legacy is not only temporary but one that will bring them closer to God and to eternity with Him.

Teaching and Modeling

Teaching and Modeling

Only be careful, and watch yourselves closely
so that you do not forget the things your eyes have seen
or let them slip from your heart as long as you live.
Teach them to your children
and to their children after them.

DEUTERONOMY 4:9

TEACHING IS ONE OF THE PRIMARY responsibilities of a Christian grandparent. Deuteronomy, chapter 4, is a scriptural mandate to teach what we have seen and know to be true from our life experiences.

We are admonished to teach children the power and beauty of friendship with God through prayer, that hard work has rewards, that God's promises are true, that mistakes can be fixed, and, in this fast-paced world, such things as kindness, manners, and helpfulness count for something. Grandparents can pass on values and Christian principles even though we are not the central authority in a child's life. We can help a child sift contentment from the static of a noisy world.

Christian grandparents teach by example that it is still true—the answers to life's questions are in God's Word. Modeling those answers in children's and grandchildren's lives is both an opportunity and a challenge.

PRAYER

Let Them See You Pray

Q. My husband is a pastor who spends a great deal of time in prayer. We both do. We have two grown children. Don't let anyone try to convince you that PKs always turn out perfect. We have one son who has caused us a lot of grief but has given us a truly perfect grandchild. He and his family do not attend church but so far have not objected to our taking our granddaughter to church with us. Sometimes, from conversation, I get the feeling our son misses the practice of faith he knew in his boyhood, but he doesn't bend.

When our granddaughter, who is five, comes to spend the night, she wants to learn how to pray. Can we teach her?

A. Tell your son that your granddaughter has asked to learn how to pray, and get his permission to teach her. If it is not given, continue to let your granddaughter see you in prayer as usual. Allow her to join you if she asks, but do not formally teach her.

Your granddaughter wants to talk to God. She longs for fellowship with Him, prompted by the Holy Spirit. Surely, with the training you and your husband provided early in his life, your son knows the innocent longing of a child to know God. Perhaps as time goes by, his heart will soften.

Pray for him. Thank the Lord for the work He is doing right now, by His grace, to restore your son's practicing faith.

Think on these words from Roberta C. Bondi's book, *To Pray and to Love:*

> For those who long for God, who seek a life of prayer
> and love, every bitter valley at last will become a place
> of springs. Human beings cannot make springs. All
> prayer, all life, all love finally are the gifts of God's

generous grace that waters the world like the rivers of Paradise. In prayer we ask God for grace to enter the kingdom of love for which we were created. Prayer prepares us for the kingdom.[1]

My prayer for you and your granddaughter is that your son will once again seek the Lord through repentant prayer and receive the living water that renews a sin-parched soul.

> Prayer is not the mystery language of the specialist
> but the heartfelt cry of the child.[2]

Praying for and with Grandchildren

Q. Both of my grandchildren are in public school and face temptation and other difficulties every day. They know I pray for them. I would appreciate any help you can offer on effective prayer for grandchildren.

A. Here are guidelines for praying for and with grandchildren:

- Pray for your grandchildren before they are conceived. Ask God to make you into the grandparent they will need.
- As the baby grows, pray for the baby's healthy development, physically, spiritually, and emotionally. Pray for wisdom and a special sensitivity toward this child.
- Thank God for protecting the infant and for giving the child a sense of security and well-being and a responsive heart toward Him.
- Pray in your grandchildren's rooms at their home. When you visit, step into their rooms and pray. God's presence can fill a place so that it affects what happens there.
- Ask God to bring your grandchildren to mind whenever they need help. As you think of them, stop for a moment of prayer,

prompted by the Holy Spirit. The more you do this, the more you will sense what they need and how to pray for them.

- Don't force a grandchild to pray in your world. First Corinthians 13:11 says that when you are a child, you think as one. Pray in their world. Pray about things that are important to them, not just teaching them a memorized prayer. When a five-year-old learns that God can help him skip rope, then as a teen, he may believe God can help him with loneliness and later with financial pressures and marriage. Positive prayer as a child strengthens faith for bigger things later in life.
- Pray *with* them rather than *at* them. If prayer is used as a means of discipline, children won't want to pray.
- Teach them to pray for others' needs, praying until the answer comes. Give thanks with them when God answers. Share your prayer needs with them. This forms a strong bond between you as they pray for you and realize that you value their prayers.
- Pray for the healing of their spirits. Ask God to help you be sensitive to their hurts and to see the hurts from their perspective. Pray for God to touch their hurt and heal it, so hurts do not build up.
- Another way to pray for grandchildren is by joining a Moms in Touch group for grandparents. Call 1-800-949-MOMS for the location of a group in your area.
- If your grandchildren are adopted or foster children, pray for every part of their lives before they became part of your family.
- Believe in their spiritual potential. Grandparents can make a big difference as they recognize and affirm their grandchildren's gifts and help develop them.
- Look for opportunities for spontaneous prayer with your grandchildren. It could well be the moment in their day that gets them through their day.[3]

TRADITIONS

Changing Traditions

Q. For years, since our two children have grown up, married, and had their own children, our home has been the destination for Easter dinner, Thanksgiving Day, and Christmas Eve. It was just understood. Our grandchildren are all school-age now, and this year, their parents have announced a new tradition of having these celebrations at their individual homes. Both my daughter and my son were kind about explaining this change to me. It's fine with my husband, and it's fine with me too. It just hurts. What will I do with myself?

A. There are family traditions that never change, and there are those that should remain flexible. The practice of faith, being there for each other, confronting one another with love, and continuing family values passed on through the generations are examples of immovable traditions. Practically speaking, however, it is nearly impossible for a family to keep customs that make one person happy to the detriment of others. One such custom is the one your letter addresses.

Do you remember what it was like when you had your young family, splitting yourself up to share with both sets of grandparents on important days? In our day, perhaps that was easier than today with stressful family schedules in a faster-paced world. The modern family tends to buck tradition when it comes to extended family celebrations in favor of establishing traditions of their own with their nuclear family. There's nothing wrong with that. In fact, it's a good idea.

What will you do with yourself? I'd say prepare to split yourself up for them because you will have invitations, I'm sure, to be with one or the other on those important days. Don't worry. You won't be left behind.

And think of all those turkeys and hams *someone else* will cook and serve!

Preserving Family History

Q. Our large family is fragmented all over the world. We have five children, seventeen grandchildren, and two greats. I have kept careful diaries of my growing up, marriage, the children, and have a pretty complete family tree that goes back five generations. Before I die, I would like to make this information available to all of the children. Do you have any thoughts on how I can accomplish this goal when we are scattered here, there, and everywhere?

A. Thank the Lord we live in the age of technology! Here are some high-tech ideas for you that won't require you to be a computer or video genius:

Gather together all of your priceless, collected information, and anecdotes. Lay them out on a long table and make chronological sense of them. Then have someone videotape you narrating the history of your family as you know it. (It doesn't have to be MGM quality; you don't have to look perfect; and if something gets out of order, don't worry about it.)

Be sure to pause often to add those heart-touching memories and funny stories of parents and grandchildren growing up. (It's OK to laugh, and it's OK to cry.) Take the viewer on a historical tour as well, if you can, adding such touches as the name of the president of the United States at the time, and note changes in geography, style, or culture.

If you're camera shy (don't be), speak your family history into a tape recorder. It may take twenty tapes. So be it.

Whichever option you choose, video or voice only, make enough copies to go around, and mail them to your children, grands, and greats. You may want to plan for Christmas, or perhaps your birthday, as a time to distribute this gesture of your thankfulness for the part each one has played in your life.

Many have regrets that we didn't think of doing something like this. Congratulations, and send me a copy!

MODELING

Kindness and Gentleness

Q. Our grandchildren, ages ten and eight, are confronted daily with rude, impolite, and hostile behavior patterns in people around them at school, in stores, and on the streets. We also observe it in the way they fight and squabble with each other at home. Do you have any ideas on how we can counteract such negative behavior, to soften their spirits and show them that kindness and gentleness are virtues worth preserving in themselves and in others?

A. Kindness and gentleness are hallmarks of God's character and should, therefore, be part of our character. Planting these virtues in grandchildren can be accomplished by grandparents in a variety of ways.

Your local Christian bookstore and your library have a wide range of books and tapes on sharing and showing kindness. Have some handy at your house. Sit and read or listen to them with your grandchildren. Give them as gifts. Reading together gives opportunity for discussion of something that happened that day or a problem the child may be having. You can show your kindness by listening to all that the child has to tell.

Marshal your grandchildren's energies into a neighborhood ministry such as baking cookies or muffins for one who has been sick, feeding a pet that has been left alone, or pulling weeds in the garden of an elderly person.

Florence Turnidge has a nursing home ministry, visiting residents with her grandchildren. During the visits, the children read Scripture and sing with the residents, demonstrating simple kindnesses such as holding a hand not held by a child for many years, placing a sticker on the back of the hand that says "I love you," or praying aloud for one of the residents. Such demonstrated kindess on the part of children has proven to make a tremendous difference in the well-being of nursing home residents.

Instill kindness by teaching your grandchildren to give unexpected presents—simple handmade gifts for parents, siblings, and friends. Help a child address and stamp a special card or letter on a birthday, anniversary, or illness of a friend or family member, all the while talking about the fact that this is what Jesus would do for someone else.

Reinforce their parents' teachings on gentleness by stressing, at every opportunity, the importance of saying "I'm sorry." For example, extending forgiveness to small children who misbehave and say they are sorry is excellent training for another time when unkind words or behavior confront them. The children will remember your example.

> What communities need first are order and safety;
> what children need above all are love and order and
> good examples.[4]

Grammar and Swearing

Q. I have a question regarding the poor language our only grandchild uses. Since she is only three-and-a-half, we are hoping we might be able to do something about it now before she gets older. Both the mother and father are college graduates, but, because of our son's work, they live in a rural community. We're sure our granddaughter picks up such words as "ain't" and phrases like "them don't" and "it don't" from her baby-sitter and her little friends. I know this concerns her parents also.

As her grandparents, how should we treat this problem we see, and how should a grandparent react to four-letter words when they pop out of a child's mouth?

A. Foul language from any child is surely not tolerated at the child's home and should not be tolerated at yours. Youngsters who come cussing should be advised to use better language or they will not be invited back again. Three-and-a-half-year-olds will pick up almost anything floating by, including bad words, and should learn, with firm direction, that those words are unacceptable.

Simple grammatical errors are not nearly so serious. Correcting each one as it comes out of a child's mouth can be done by using the right words yourself:

"It don't go, Grandma!"

Response: "It doesn't go? Here, I'll fix it."

"Git it for me!"

Response: "All right, dear, I'll get it for you."

Praise her successes, ignore mistakes. Over time, as she grows, she will learn from her parent's training and by your example. In school, reading, writing, and good grades will teach her the value and correctness of good language.

Support her parents by encouraging them to relax about your granddaughter's grammar lapses and concentrate on teaching good, solid values that will form the person she is to be, a person who will know the difference between right and wrong, in words and in life.

The Work Ethic

Q. Am I wrong or does it seem like kids are just plain lazy today? My grandsons are thirteen and fourteen and would sit around all night if I let them. I'm their grandfather, and I baby-sit them at their house while my divorced daughter works the night shift at the hospital. I asked one of them to take out the garbage, and you'd think I'd asked for the moon! Such small chores eventually get done, but not when I ask. They'd rather watch TV or play games on the computer. It's OK with me that they entertain themselves this way, but how about helping out sometimes?

They mind pretty well when it comes to homework, eating what's put in front of them, and getting to bed. They just seem to be lazy.

When I was a kid, I worked. We had a farm that was in the family for generations, and if you've been around one, you know everybody has to do his share. We knew that was expected of us; we wouldn't have thought of it any other way. My daughter and her brothers also learned to work hard. Today's kids, especially teenagers, don't seem to have that strong work ethic my generation grew up with. I've had friends say the same thing about their grandkids, so I know it's not just mine that have this problem.

A. Teenagers today live stressful lives. They work hard in different ways than you and I did when we were young. The out-of-home demands on their time combined with the pressures of being almost grown-up can be daunting.

However, every teenager needs structure at home. A plan. Goals and objectives they can strive for and accomplish. That's the way it is in the outside world they are scrambling to fit into.

Their home environment needs to be a safe place where they can regroup, but it should also require that same striving to be the best they can be as adulthood beckons.

The problem you are experiencing stems from the obvious fact that your daughter has not passed on the work ethic you taught her so well. There's no plan, no expectation, no structure. Now, she might be handling the boys that way for a reason. She may not expect a lot from them at home for the very reason that their schedules are so packed. Find out.

Have a chat with her about her childhood the next time you get a chance. Think of ways you can help her to help your grandsons respond better and to be better helpers around the house. Listen to her. Hear her out. Then the two of you come up with a plan and a promise that both of you will enforce it.

Self-esteem, simply defined, means "how you feel about yourself." Your grandsons need some lessons on how to build a healthy self-esteem and a healthy reputation by pitching in and sharing chores and being more attentive to the needs of others.

Congratulations on being a good dad, helping your daughter in the critical role of sitter. You can partner with her now to help your grandsons grow to responsible adulthood and take better care of the love and nurture you provide them out of the goodness of your heart.

Letting Them Help

Q. Both our son and daughter do a good job assigning chores at home, and it seems to be paying off handsomely. Our three grandchildren are well behaved and industrious. How can I foster the same good ideals when they are at my house, which is quite often?

A. At your house, make a game of it. At home, it's expected. Let it be more fun at Grandma's.

Even small children can learn to make their own beds in the morning after a sleep-over. If it's not perfect, compliment them anyway. See that visiting grandchildren hang up their own clothes. Lower clothes rods in one closet so little ones can reach. Keep empty drawers children can call their own when they come to stay. Give lots of compliments for keeping things in apple-pie order and for saving time to do things with you that are a lot more fun.

Have a special box for each child to store toys. Decorate the box with the child's name, and put it where the child can find it easily. This makes picking up toys easier. Keep a footstool in your bathroom and one in the kitchen so small children can reach to brush their teeth or get a cup. In my kitchen, small grandchildren know that the second drawer holds disposable cups for drinks of water. They get a cup themselves, serve their own water, and throw the cup away.

Teach your grandchildren to wipe the sink after using it, fold their towels, and hang them back on the rack. Specify that decorator towels in the bathroom are not to be used, or they will be—count on it!

Good for you, Grandma! You are helping your grandchildren grow with a sense of responsibility and accomplishment and the joy that comes from pleasing you!

Negative Teaching

Q. I read in your study course, *Grandparenting by Grace*, about the grandfather who drank and, at his funeral, his grandson said, "I learned a lot from Grandpa. I learned how *not* to live." That really got to me because I think I've been doing a lot of things wrong.

I came from a poor family. We never had much. There was a lot of hollering and hitting. When I got married to a fine Christian woman, we all went to church and studied the Bible. I hollered at my son, however, and told him he was no good, just like my dad did to me. Now, I hear him yelling a blue streak at my ten-year-old grandson, and I can hardly stand it.

I know it's my fault, but I'm a proud man. There's nothing I can do about it, but it nearly kills me to watch it and know I'm the one responsible for it. Also, I'm having regrets about all the suffering I caused my wife.

A. There *is* something you can do about it, and you need to do it *now*. In God's Word, in 1 Corinthians 10:13, is a promise that God will never allow a difficult circumstance in your life without allowing you a way to get out of it. The way to undo negative teaching is to honestly repent of it. Tell God you're sorry, and ask His forgiveness. Then go to your dad, if you can, and tell him you forgive him for hollering and hitting you when you were young. If your dad has passed away, pray a prayer of forgiveness.

Then go to your son and apologize for yelling at him when he was a boy. Ask his forgiveness and try to convince him to change the pattern of verbal abuse he is perpetuating as a father. Tell him you'll help him. Then both of you go to your grandson and have a talk with him. Tell your grandson about your upbringing and how you continued this bad behavior because that's all you knew, but that, from now on, it is going to be different with his dad and better.

Then you need to ask forgiveness from your wife. She will be thrilled about it, and you will lift a heavy burden from her heart that she has carried a long time. The last step is to forgive yourself.

These are not easy steps for you and your son to take, and it will be emotional for all of you. But it must be done and now.

Negative teaching is like the locusts in the Book of Joel. It devours and destroys the fruit of a loving relationship, but God promises to repay you for the years the locust has eaten. He will erase the past sins and never let it happen again. Trust Him, and begin the healing process today while you still have time to make it right.

Fixing Mistakes

Q. I had a rude awakening the other night when I overheard my own daughter say to my sixteen-year-old granddaughter, "Just tell them part of it. They don't need to know the whole truth. That's the way Grandma and Grandpa operate."

I was floored, but I realized she was right. Looking back over the years, both of us have done so much wrong as parents. Now that our daughter is grown and has our grandchildren, how can we undo some of the damage? I know it will take time.

A. We can't change what has already happened. What you *can* do is begin to talk openly with your daughter about your mistakes. Be brutally honest about everything. Don't be afraid. It will bring you much closer to your daughter and keep her from making the same mistakes. You will also be helping your grandchild, and that is your primary job at this season of life.

Be glad you overheard the truth. It was your wake-up call.

God loves you just the way you are.
But He loves you too much to leave you that way.

Mentoring

Q. Our son married at seventeen and has a darling little boy we adore. My concern is the child's mother, our daughter-in-law, who is only twenty now, and comes from a broken family. She knows little or nothing about keeping a house, cooking, or raising a child. We've yet to be invited for dinner, although they come here often. My husband and I watch them muddle through. What do you suppose I might do to help her without being intrusive?

A. You have a perfect setting for mentoring. A mentor is a trusted counselor, guide, tutor, or coach.

Begin by asking your daughter-in-law, in a loving, nonthreatening way, if she would like to try a relationship like that. You will need her approval. Then make plans for times you can get together. Attend interior design shows. Your local public power utility has a home economist on staff and may offer free seminars on cooking and baking. Spend time in your kitchen and in hers with tried-and-true recipes and a large measure of patience.

Tell her how it was for you and your husband when you first started out in marriage. Laugh together about some of the mistakes each of you has made.

Be cautious about instruction regarding the raising of your grandson. Gently teach on mothering by sharing with her your own experience raising her husband. That can be lots of fun too. Show her how to build your grandson's self-esteem, how to reward him for doing chores, and how to keep him clean and healthy.

Always keep your place as mother-in-law and friend; don't overstep your boundaries or force any issues. That could be disastrous. Let her know you are as near as the telephone if she wants to talk to you, and that you will respond quickly.

The rewards of mentoring a daughter-in-law are many. Everyone benefits. You take grandparenting to new heights as a mentor, and you will deepen a bond of friendship and gratitude that will last a lifetime.

For additional insight on the mentoring relationship, read Esther Burroughs' new book, *A Garden Path to Mentoring, Planting Your Life in Another, Releasing the Fragrance of Christ*, published by New Hope.

PRINCIPLES

Christian Principles for Teens

Q. Our teenage grandson attends a public school that is notorious for gang fights, drugs, and truancy. He has a good, Christian home, but we are noticing the conflict he has between what he knows to be true and what he is living with at school and with his friends. He is especially close to my husband, and the questions he is asking his grandfather when they are together show that he could easily slip away from his Christian beliefs as he becomes older. Do you have any suggestions to help us strengthen his faith without preaching to him? He would not respond to that.

A. Teens are especially vulnerable to backsliding in today's culture. Often, confused teenagers will rebel against the teachings of a parent, the central authority figure in their lives. For the simple reason that they are *not* the central authority figure in the child's life, wise grandparents can step in and teach teens when they don't even know they're being taught.

The greatest task we grandparents have is to send sound messages about Christianity to our grandchildren by how we live our lives. *Force-fed faith will be rejected by teenagers.*

- *Prove* God's love by recounting all He has done for you.
- *Validate* His mercy by telling real-life stories of His intervention and care.
- *Demonstrate* that God's promises are true by sharing the many ways He has blessed you and your family during your lifetime of obedience to biblical instruction.

- *Affirm* for your teenage grandchild, by the gusto with which you live your own life, that living as a Christian leads to an exciting life.

Spiritual Truths

Q. One of my many treasured memories from childhood is my grandfather playing "congregation" while my two sisters and I, none of us over ten, conducted the "service" from the top porch step. He made sure we started with a central Scripture verse, such as one of the Beatitudes or "For God so loved the world . . . ." I always got to hold the Bible because I was the oldest girl. I remember reading God's Word as best I could, looking down at Grandpa's attentive, lined, weathered, wonderful face, knowing in my heart that this must be important to me or it wouldn't be so important to Grandpa. These "pretend church services" helped me and my sisters feel more comfortable with God's Word. We loved our Grandpa, and we knew he loved the Lord.

My dear husband would have been such a grandfather, but he passed away before getting to know our two grandchildren. Do you have any ideas that will help me to instill spiritual values and truths in these precious grandchildren and continue my grandfather's legacy?

A. One grandmother plans a mini-devotion for her grandchild when she knows he is coming to visit. Her Bible, old and well used, is always visible in the living room, and her nine-year-old grandson makes a beeline for it now. When she started this ritual four years ago, she began by talking him through the preliminary pages of her family Bible, showing marriages, births and deaths, and explaining carefully who each person was and is. This was her way of passing on family history. Then, as he grew, she began with favorite verses from her childhood, allowing her grandson to read every other line as he was able. The devotion was brief but had three purposes: (1) to spend close personal time with her grandson, (2) to familiarize him with God's Word, and (3) to teach him how to seek out answers to his questions.

Another grandmother goes over her sermon notes from Sunday service on Monday afternoon with her fifteen-year-old granddaughter.

Still another says that when she has her little ones at the mall, they spend time in the Christian bookstore, listening to tapes, watching a video, or poring over books and puzzles.

Holidays are good times to reinforce spiritual truths. Let your gifts be spiritually uplifting: a children's Bible versus another outfit, the story of the Cross at Easter instead of another bunny or painted egg, a homemade Christmas card depicting the love of Jesus instead of one more toy. When you do buy that outfit or fun gift for a grandchild, tuck in a Christian bookmark or stickers that tell a spiritual truth.

Along with the Bible, read with your grandchildren books that tell stories of the great missionaries, famous Christian leaders, and the unique truths they espoused. Take every opportunity to read with your grand-children.

Answer their questions by asking a question in return:

"Grandma, do I hurt God's feelings when I'm bad?"

"Well, how do you think it makes God feel when you do something bad?"

Asking a question in response to children's questions helps them think out their own answers rather than have you spoon-feed a conclusion to them. However, when a specific question arises about biblical truths–such as "Who is God?" or "Where do I go when I die?" or "What does salvation mean?"—it is a grandparent's duty to give full and complete answers. Even small children, who may have trouble understanding the full explanation, will bank the information in their memory for later with-drawal.

Playing games with the Bible is a fun way to teach spiritual truths. Looking up favorite Scriptures in competition with a sibling is a self-esteem builder and a learning session all in one.

Take them to church with you, or accompany them with their parents. Family unity in a church service speaks loud and clear to children that the people whom they love have love for God and His truths.

Successful grandparents don't *preach* spiritual truths. They *live* them before a grandchild's eyes and instill them into their hearts in creative, thoughtful ways that they can pass on to their children.

Your Influence

Q. Something happened this past Christmas that taught me how much even the little things can matter to a grandchild. For fifteen years, I have baked three kinds of Christmas cookies for our large family celebration at my daughter's house. I'm getting on in years and get pretty tired by the end of the day, so I announced that I would be making only the Snickerdoodles and the Choco-boats and would skip the Pecan Smoothies. Well, my young grandson had a fit. "You have to make the Pecan Smoothies, Grannie! They're my favorites! It just won't be Christmas if you don't make your special Pecan Smoothies!"

He never had told me they were his favorites! But I sure did learn it that day. Of course, I made them, and I learned that grandkids don't always show you what's important to them. I guess I just need to keep doing what I'm doing.

A. What you learned is a lesson for us all! If a grandson harbors a secret love for your Pecan Smoothies, how much more does he love you? Children are like learning sponges for the ones they love and the ones they know love them. He may not tell you often or at all, but finding it out in this way gives you the blessed opportunity to enlarge your influence in his life.

Let your Smoothies open wide the door to a new and deeper friendship with your grandson. Teach him about family history, and tell him the many ways God has helped you in your long life. Grab those opportunities to be a positive influence in his life.

He loves you more than he loves your cookies.

Grandchildren and Their Siblings

LOVE

BEHAVIOR

JOURNALING

TOUCHING

Grandchildren and Their Siblings

*I never knew I could love anyone
the way I love this child!*

THE BOND BETWEEN GRANDPARENT and child is one of the most treasured family relationships. Most grandparents feel it from the day a baby is born, even before, and somehow, we just know the baby feels it too.

The Blessings of Grandbabies

- Anticipation of the birth
- The first look at the miracle
- Holding your own grandchild in your arms
- The memory-jogging scent of baby powder
- That first smile meant just for you
- Dimpled fingers, toes, and elbows
- The privilege of watching them grow

Blessings increase as the years go by and as we grow into our new identity: Nana, Grammie, Poppie, Meemaw, Peepah, Gammaw—the name that forever changes who we are and our status in the family. Then number one gets a baby sister or brother, and the cycle of pure joy repeats itself as we settle in for the golden journey of our lifetime—a journey of discovery, responsibility, and love enough to help each grandchild grow according to God's plan.

The questions in section 4 verify that grandparents are not perfect people. Grandchildren are not perfect either—but they go home with their parents!

LOVE

Ten Ways to Love Your Grandchildren

Q. We have ten marvelous grandchildren, some who live in loving Christian homes and some who have unfortunately experienced the divorce of their parents. Each child is different from the others. They are uniquely individual and special. How can we love them all the same when their needs are so different?

A. Grandchildren draw their conclusions about how loved they are from your response to them, and what you do is more important than what you say. Show your heart to each grandchild by responding to their passions, fears, strengths, and failings in these ten ways:

1. Accept your grandchildren for who they are. You ask a grandchild a question, and he looks at his shoes and says nothing. You expect more from him than that. Accept that your expectation of him at that moment might be too high or even misguided.

   You planned a nice afternoon at the zoo only to discover your grandchild has absolutely no interest in seeing the animals. Well-meaning grandparents can inadvertently damage a grandchild's self-esteem by conveying, however slightly, their displeasure or disappointment. Show that in your heart there's room for kids who don't, kids who won't, and kids who can't—that how you feel about them is not touched by their performance. Rather than impose your thoughts or feelings, try to track the source of the behavior and understand it.

2. Encourage their strengths. Turn what might be considered character flaws into attributes. For example, when a grandchild takes a chance and it doesn't work out, call it courageous, not foolhardy. It's more loving to say a grandchild is a leader rather than bossy, gentle rather than wimpy, laid-back rather than lazy.

3. Understand their age bracket. Try to rush a toddler grandchild, and they become overwhelmed. The preteen's emerging value system is reinforced for good when grandparents love them through the right and the wrong. A teenager is caught between childhood and adulthood and needs your stability and consistency.

4. Spend time with them. I believe scheduling one-on-one time with a grandchild is as important as a doctor or dentist appointment. Put it on your calendar, and follow through.

5. Listen. Listen. Listen. It's a noisy world. Be the one they can come to and unload on, and be sure they know that all of it is safe with you. Grandchildren who need to talk to someone will come to their own conclusions if a faithful listener allows them to lay out what is on their minds. No psychology degree is necessary. Just love.

6. Keep commitments. Grandchildren, especially those who have been through traumatic relationships at home, will feel let down by everyone at times. If a plan is made, stick to it. Keep promises, even if it hurts. Let your grandchild know that, without a doubt, you are as good as your word, according to God's Word. "Then they believed his promises and sang his praise" (Psalm 106:12).

7. Respect your grandchildren's choices. "She's not going to the college from which you and your daughter graduated!" "He

married *that* girl?" Parents lay the foundation; children make the choices. Our job is to stand with our grandchildren without reproach but showing love no matter their choices in life. Then if the choice turns out to be wrong, who is it they will come to for advice and counsel?

8. Set and honor limits. Lack of parental control and lack of discipline in any home environment can cause a grandchild to test our limits. Leniency to the misbehaving grandchild is like giving them a license to push for more. Every child needs definition of what he may or may not do. Once a rule or boundary is set, stick to it and be ready to explain why, patiently and with tough love.

9. Have fun together. At home there are rules all the time. Help your grandchildren enjoy life when they are with you by displaying an attitude of joy, exploration, or adventure—whatever fits your personality. Relax with them as you share who you are and revel in their free spirits.

10. Model your Christian faith. There is no greater gift a grandparent can give than to teach a grandchild to love God and His principles. A legacy of money and things pales in comparison to the eternal value of a closer walk with the Savior.

BEHAVIOR

When Grandchildren Come to Visit

Q. I'm new at this grandparenting game since I inherited two grandchildren in my daughter's recent marriage. They live with their mother in another city. They are adorable children, seven and nine, but we don't know each other very well yet. I want to do a good job when they come to visit us for the first time in a couple of weeks. They'll be with us for ten days! Any ideas to help us all relax and get to know each other better will be appreciated. Thanks!

A.   A good way to start planning a visit from grandchildren is to let them be part of the planning. Help them to anticipate the time and getting to know you by asking them about special things they would like to do or places they'd like to see while they are with you. You can do this by phone or letter. Sometimes a letter is best, because you can punctuate it with stars, hearts, or exclamation points that help build excitement. (Be careful not to build their expectations too high.)

When they arrive, give them time to settle into their new surroundings before involving them in activities. Hugs and kisses might be out of place, depending on how well you know the children and how well they know you. Don't shower them with gifts unless they have to do with plans you've already made together, such as a pennant for their favorite team you're going to root for or a book about animals you plan to see.

Include them in your normal daily routine. If you usually go to the market on a certain day, go ahead and do that, taking them with you. If wash day is every Monday, ask them to set out dirty clothes Sunday night.

Be patient and understanding with their moods. One child may react differently from another, throwing the schedule into turmoil. Don't be hurt, and don't coax. Adjust and relax. Be ready with some alternate plans. Sometimes a child just wants to "hang around" and do nothing.

Teach them something while you have them—perhaps a new skill, a sport, or family history. In your case, it would be interesting and important for the step-grandchildren to learn more about you and your family.

Create one tradition that becomes yours alone, something only the four of you do together. Something they can take back with them, remember fondly, and look forward to on another visit.

Take lots of pictures and videos that capture their visit. Send copies home with them, and make an album of the visit for your coffee table in the living room. Next time they come, you can add to the memories.

The Dangers of Favoritism

Q.   Our two granddaughters are opposites. One is shy and reserved. She doesn't like to play games or go out with us but prefers reading books alone. She is warm and loving, just not outgoing. Her sister chatters like a magpie, has boundless energy, and showers my husband with affection.

We are blessed to have them both. The problem is that Grandpa shows definite favoritism to the granddaughter who openly adores him. She's real good at getting what she wants from him, and he encourages it while practically ignoring the quiet one. I've noticed lately that it is affecting my sweet, shy granddaughter. She is withdrawing, and her parents are asking how it could be that she doesn't get excited about coming over to our house anymore. Well, I know why. She loves her Grandpa and isn't getting loved back. She knows her sister gets all the attention.

What should I say to my husband?

A. Tell your husband exactly what's going on, and do it right away. He may not be aware of his overt favoritism, but he needs to make new efforts to show love to his shy granddaughter.

Consider separating the time the girls spend with Grandpa. He needs to spend equal time to discover the wonderful differences in the two and how to react in a loving, grandfatherly way to each.

Children who are ignored or sense that they are not favored by grandparents suffer greatly. Sometimes the feelings will be just under the surface and never spoken. Sometimes a child's behavior will say everything about what is going on. They may question, "What's wrong with me that I am not picked to do things or go places with my grandparent? Am I a bad person?" When a grandparent spends time with a child, but he doesn't have his heart in it, the grandchild can feel it and wonders why.

Scripture tells us that our children's children are a crown to the aged. Responsibility comes with the crown. When attention is not freely given equally, the result can be permanent personality damage and loss of self-esteem. For girls, how their grandfather treats them affects their developing thoughts about men in general as they grow older.

Sensitivity to doing our utmost for the psychological well-being of our grandchildren is part of the responsibility that comes with the crown.

Telling Jokes

Q. My husband has a habit of telling jokes to our two grandchildren. Most of the time they are OK, and the children get a kick out of them and expect to hear a funny joke every time they are together. But every so often, a joke will be off-color, maybe just a little bit. Once in a while, they are just not appropriate at all. I can't tell you what some of them have been, but I see the reaction of my grandchildren as they look really uncomfortable.

I'm concerned that they might lose a little respect for their grandfather, who is really a terrific person. How can I get him to realize that some of his jokes might not be appropriate for children?

A. Simply tell him. "Dear, the kids love you. They don't love some of your jokes when they get a little off-color. Inappropriate jokes confuse their young minds, and I know you don't want to be any part of causing that."

Your approach needs to be loving and nonaccusatory but to the point. If he continues with this practice, tell him again. Your husband may be unaware of this offensive habit. Give him the benefit of the doubt, but put a stop to it now.

The Pitfalls of Perfectionism

Q. I heard a special message last Sunday from a visiting speaker whose words touched me deeply and forced me to recognize a few things about myself.

I grew up in a strict, authoritarian home. I always knew what was expected of me and the consequences if I didn't measure up. Mine was not a happy childhood, and I'm afraid I raised my two children with the same regimented lifestyle. I have regrets about it, and now that I am a grand-mother, I want to try to accept the grandchildren, ages one and four, as they are and hope that they can care for me as well. How should I proceed?

A. Old, ingrained habits are hard to break. Thank God for the visiting speaker who was sent to help you start a whole new chapter in your life as a happy, contented grandmother!

As a Christian grandmother, you will want to model Christ's behavior for your grandchildren. Striving for perfection in that role will fail, for there is only one perfect Person.

The best any of us can do is our best.

Expecting perfection from grandchildren will also result in failure. Rigidity in family life, a judgmental attitude, and perfectionism wrecks relationships. A young mother wrote saying she felt she could no longer take her young daughter to see her grandmother. Almost every time they were together, the grandmother made a critical remark such as, "Why are you in red? You know you look better in pink!" or "Get your hair out of that silly ponytail! It's much better down on your shoulders." This grand-mother's critical attitude caused great harm all around, especially to the young girl's self-esteem. That was too much for the young mother to take, so the relationship was restricted. Everyone lost.

Psychologist Dan Montgomery reminds us that grandparents learn two of life's greatest lessons: "that loving relationships are the spiritual goal of life and that patience with children's shortcomings helps them gradually mature. And wise are the grandparents who recognize, according to Proverbs 17:6, that grandchildren are the crown of their later years."[1]

You know these truths now. Go to your children, explaining that you have been repeating a negative family pattern and have regrets about it. Talking with them will be a relief for all of you as you step together into a better life.

Be careful not to step into the blaming department or the house of deep regret. Your eyes have been opened! You will have a loving and fruitful grandparenting season.

Better to spend an entire day in prayer
than to spend it striving for perfection.

Living with Their Fads

Q. On a recent visit to our daughter's home, we were appalled at the appearance of our teenage grandson. He's had the barber fashion his high-school letters into his haircut. One side of his hair is long, the other is short. He's got a stringy ponytail down his back, and his clothes are mismatched and raggedy looking. What are we supposed to do or say when confronted with a grandchild who looks like that?

A. What, no earring? No nose ring? Be grateful he hasn't adopted some of the more severe fads like the belly button ring or the diamond stud embedded in the tongue. Today's kids are under peer pressure such as you and I have never known.

Who is that boy underneath the haircut and the outfit? I think, if you look closely, you'll see he's the same one you've been crazy about all these years. He's embraced a trend, a fad that will pass. He's trying to fit in with his friends. He's trying something new. Often, an attitude goes with the attire, an attitude that causes problems at home, but you have no control there unless your advice is sought. Your job as a grandparent is to understand and have patience with your grandson.

Avoid criticizing him. The child rebuffed by family will often go to further extremes just to prove individuality. Chiding can backfire on both parents and grandparents.

Do not compliment him, lending credence to his looks. That could get you in hot water with his parents, who are probably trying to get him to change. Do not take sides with the boy, especially against his parents' expressed concern over his current style. Take your cues from his parents. They are in charge and need your support.

Your understanding, patience, and love could be an example that helps turn your grandson from "weird" back into just plain "cool."

Sibling Rivalry at Grandma's

Q. When I have the grandchildren, I've noticed more and more squabbling, aggression, and outright war between them. They are boys, ages eight and ten. The older boy delights in teasing his little brother unmercifully, sending him crying to me, taking his special toys and hiding them, and hitting far too hard. The younger one knows how to push his big brother's buttons and does so every chance he gets. He will ruin something his brother has made, for example, and then run. He taunts and shouts loudly. When they get even, they really hurt each other, get very angry, and lash out with all their might. It's like they hate each other!

This is also a big problem at home, and my daughter is asking for help. They have a normal, loving Christian home environment. I've been reading up on attention deficit disorder. We wonder, is this just a phase that will pass, or do we have a problem?

A. With two or more children in a family, it is quite likely that there will be some degree of bickering or arguing. This behavior can be a good thing as two children learn to assert themselves and get along over a period of time. However, a pattern of long-term negative behavior, especially escalating to physical harm, bears looking into by the parents. You are a good grandma to inquire.

Researchers have suggested a number of reasons for siblings to develop serious relationship problems: The parents may show favoritism that sparks resentment in one child who takes it out on the other; the older child may feel replaced by the younger; or one child may be living in the shadow of the achievements of a more talented sibling.

Here are some tips for dealing with sibling rivalry:

- Avoid comparing one child with another.
- Spend quality time with each of the children.
- Encourage separate experiences and friends.

- Try to ignore disagreements and let the children learn to work these problems out by themselves.[2]

However, according to psychologist Thomas Phelan, when you do intervene, it is best to discipline both children rather than just one as each child has a way of provoking the other in ways you may not see.

When children are fighting, never ask, "Who started it?" or "What happened?" When you do, the response will usually be, "He did" or "No, she did," etc. Do not expect the older child to act in a more mature fashion than the younger child during conflict. The best option is to separate the siblings for a forced time out. You may wish to act as a referee, helping each child present their point of view and working out a compromise. It is also helpful to offer a reward that must be earned by both children.[3]

For information on attention deficit hyperactivity disorder (AD/HD) write CH.A.D.D (Children and Adults with Attention Deficit Disorders), 499 NW 70th Avenue, Suite 101, Plantation, FL 33317.

Something Important Is Missing

Q. My daughter and son-in-law complain that I am not involved in their lives. I work, and I also serve as a political volunteer in my community. I just can't get over there to see my grandson as often as they would like. How can I make them understand?

A. I don't know what you consider "often" to be. But I do know how much it can hurt parents and grandchildren when a grandparent is not involved in their lives. One little fellow told me, "My Grandma is great. She's a lot of fun, but she's too busy to see me very much. I miss her a lot." He gave a word picture of the loss that children feel when a grandparent is inconsistent or unavailable.

You are facing a difficult challenge to find the right balance between work and relationships. I encourage you to consider examining your daily routine to see if "often" might be increased. Think on these questions: Which is more important to you—your work or your family? Who can take your place with your grandchild? Also, realize the importance of how we model for our adult children. What example are you living for your daughter?

The fact that your daughter has expressed her feelings speaks volumes about her pain. She misses you, and you are missing out on one of the most cherished bondings in a family—the grandparent/grandchild relationship.

Most important perhaps, your grandchild needs you. Share your interesting, wonderful self with him. He'll grow up quicker than you can say, "Sorry, I can't come over," and you might have some questions to answer.

We all set examples by our lives. It is healthy to check up on priorities once in a while. Maybe this is your time to do so. I know hundreds of long-distance grandparents who would gladly trade places with you.

JOURNALING

Write Down What They Say and Do

Q. I suppose you hear this from every grandparent, but our grandchildren say and do the cutest things. Any ideas on remembering them, so I can share them with others? They happen and then I can't remember them!

A. Write it down, Grandma! Some grandparents have several boxes of corners of paper and cards and backs of programs on which they've written the wonderful things their grandchildren did or said. Scribble on anything handy before the thought gets away.

Journaling what they say and do is lots of fun. Done with love and consistency, this record will be a blessing for generations to come. Why not start today?

Audio and videotape recordings of grandchildren are another way to preserve matchless moments with grandchildren. Keep the camcorder rolling when the kids are over, or place an audiotape recorder in a strategic corner when baby-sitting. Recordings make great presents for parents. Have fun!

What to Do with Your Journal

Q. I was thinking about gathering together all the little notes I've made over the years about my granddaughter and giving them to her in some form for her eighteenth birthday. We mean a lot to each other, and she has said some really cute things and has accomplished quite a lot in her life already.

I don't know how to start and would appreciate your help. I live alone and am seventy-eight.

A. Good for you! Don't hide them in a closet or drawer, only to be found when you're gone. Putting your treasured notations in some form will result in a keepsake your granddaughter will never forget!

Ask your adult child to help you type them up into a keepsake book. It doesn't have to be fancy. The stationery store has pretty books with empty pages if you care to handwrite your gems. Otherwise you can gather typed samples together, pasting them in a scrapbook with dates alongside. Include pictures you have saved, and write your own comments next to them. Or you can simply paste them on plain paper, make a cover of a sheet of colored paper, punch holes in the left side, and bind them with ribbon or yarn.

You might even consider sending some of the special things your grandchild has said or done to the local newspaper as a way of honoring her as she turns eighteen. Give some to your church office for printing in the newsletter.

This will be a unique gift to the child's parents as well if you can make a copy. If you can do that, make one for yourself too! Such a book, placed in a strategic spot in your house or carried in a purse or pocket, would be just another way to show the world how much you love and honor your granddaughter.

It's a wonderful idea. You'll be glad you did it!

TOUCHING

Tickling

Q. I watch my husband tickle my granddaughter, and it makes me cringe. When I was little, my father used to tickle me without mercy until I couldn't breathe. I would end up crying, and he would call me a cry-baby. It's not that bad with these two, but I don't really think my granddaughter likes it. What do you think of tickling?

A. There's a difference between a gentle, occasional teasing and unmerciful tickling. Light tickling is OK, but tickling that goes too far is dangerous and humiliating; dangerous because it can cause fear, humiliating because it implies one person has a right to hold another person's body hostage, and that is not the image of a grandfather that grandchildren should have.

It's not good for you, either, because you have to watch it, and it brings back bad memories for you. If you haven't already done so, tell your husband about your experience as a child. That should be enough to stop a loving husband once he sees the damage he may be doing.

Healthy Touching

Q. The parents of my only granddaughter, who is eight years old, have done a good job of teaching her not to talk to strangers, not to get into a strange car, and what to do if somebody tries to grab her in a mall or somewhere. That's fine. I understand all that, but all this teaching has affected my closeness with her. She's not affectionate with me. She used to be when she was younger. Lately when she starts to give me a hug or a kiss, she'll move away, as though she is remembering that it is not an OK thing to do.

Can parents go too far in what they teach their kids about touching? I'm a grandpa who really misses getting a hug once in a while, and giving one too.

A. Today's societal ills and dangers cause some parents to be overly cautious about keeping their children safe from harm. Better that they err as too strict rather than too lenient! Who can blame them, as thousands of children are being snatched from malls, sidewalks, parks, and even their own bedrooms?

In America, the pattern of child abuse in the last two decades has reached frightening and shameful proportions. It's natural for parents to be alarmed and react with stern control.

Try to understand their concern. I'm sure you share it. I suggest you have a talk with your adult child about how you feel, saying that you miss the closeness you once had with your granddaughter. See if things won't loosen up a bit.

When I included the issue of healthy touching in one of the *Grandparenting by Grace* church study lessons, I did so after much prayer. I was affirmed in writing about it, however, because in the first six months following publication of the course, six Christian grandparents sought me out to tell me of accusations of improper touching of a child on their part or on the part of another family member. Unfortunately, these things do occur in Christian homes; we must accept that parents are on guard. And rightly so.

Continue to show your love to your granddaughter. My prayer for you is that, after you talk with her parents, you can get back to showing that love by healthy touches. Whether by butterfly kisses, Eskimo kisses, hugs, holding hands, cuddling up together in the rocking chair—grandparents should *always* be an example to a child of joyful, healthy touching.

Family Relationships

Your Children

Daughters and Daughters-in-Law

Sons and Sons-in-Law

The Other Grandparents

GREAT-GRANDPARENTING

HEROES

Family Relationships

Whatever life holds for you and your family
in the coming days, weave the unfailing fabric
of God's Word through your heart and mind.
It will hold strong, even if the rest of life unravels.

GIGI GRAHAM TCHIVIDJIAN

THE IDEAL FAMILY WOULD HAVE A SHARED spirituality, a fierce loyalty and genuine affection for one another, and agreed-upon, common goals of harmony, helpfulness, and gratitude. Sadly, few such families exist today.

Section 5 deals with the reality of contemporary family relationships. As we approach the next century, millions of families are fighting the second Civil War, which began in the 1960s. The lines of previously well-defined family roles have been bloodied in the battle, and families are struggling to confront their problems and heal their wounds. Grandparents are on the front lines, dedicating their lives to retrieving and nurturing God-ordained family relationships in the fervent hope that a healthy family will emerge victorious.

Grandparents have always been there, down through the centuries, ready with advice and counsel to help a daughter, a son, the in-laws, and the outlaws. Grandparents know that the basics of family relationships are still alive. Bloodied? Yes. Beaten? No. The emotional bonds of family unity, even stretched to the limit, still lie just beneath the surface of the foibles, poor choices, questionable traits, and feuds. Grandparents are living a pivotal role in the restoration of the family as God intended it. Oh, some of us make mistakes along the way, but we fight the good fight, and we're never too old to learn.

YOUR CHILDREN

Treating Your Child as an Adult

Q. I have been hurt by my twenty-seven-year-old daughter, and this time, I don't deserve it! I was trying to help my grandson, who goes to kindergarten. This afternoon when I stopped by, my daughter told me that she loves me but I should go home, that I couldn't come in. Then she slammed the door in my face.

I admit that sometimes I tend to overdo, but kids need a lot of help these days. I live a block away, and every Monday I go over and straighten the house for her after she goes to work. She doesn't have time for that. I usually fix something up for dinner for the three of them and put it in the fridge. Wednesdays I do her laundry, except lately it's been done when I get there. I try to stop by with some fresh fruit, pastries, or a casserole every day and tend to the rose bushes I planted there in the front yard. I call my little grandson every night. I pretend I'm the sandman, and he just loves it.

This morning the weather turned colder, and I just knew my daughter hadn't put a warm coat on my grandson, so I went over and got his heavy jacket from his closet and took it to the school office for him. That's what brought on this tiff. She's furious with me! But somebody's got to think of these things. I was just helping, but she takes everything the wrong way. What can I do about this? She used to be my sweet little girl! I'm just sick at her ingratitude.

A. That's not ingratitude your daughter is exhibiting. She's feeling smothered by your incessant invasion of her family's life! Your daughter is a wife and a mother, not your dependent little girl. Allow her freedom to do her own housework unless she asks for help. Let her cook for her own family. Let her make her own way, mistakes and all.

The action that struck the final blow to your daughter's tolerance was your blatant takeover of her authority over and responsibility for her son.

Grandparents cannot usurp the rightful authority of the parents. Our job is to partner with the parents in helping the child grow. Grandparents are not the central authority figure in their grandchild's life. I'm sure you can see that now.

It has been said that only puppets need strings. When parents of adult children are able to cut the strings that bind, the children can become the kind of people they want to be, and an extraordinary thing happens: Parent and child become friends; sometimes peers right away, sometimes mentor and learner, but friends on the same adult level. That can still happen for you and your daughter. Cut the strings.

Telephone your heartfelt apology to your daughter. (Don't go over again in person yet.) Tell her you are sorry and that from now on, you will come over only when asked. Promise her that, in the future, you will be a better friend and a grandmother who knows her place.

Once that is accomplished, start to switch your focus from your daughter's family to yourself and your own life. Take up some new interests, perhaps at church or in the community. Obviously, you have a lot of energy and much to give.

Your daughter will always be your girl. Parenting never stops. As a grandparent, however, meddling is something that should never begin.

Loving Unlovely Children

Q. We are a family whose Christianity was not just a Sunday experience but a way of life—living the way we believed Christians should live. We home schooled our son and daughter, prayed with them, and always tried to be a godly example. Many times other young people shared fun times with us in our home.

Somewhere along the line, though, things began to fall apart. Through the teen years, both children served the Lord in church. Then our son became involved with some neighborhood hoodlums who started him on marijuana and a long road of trouble and heartbreak from heavier drugs. But it got worse! Our daughter, now in her twenties, went crazy, living with an older man and having our first two grandchildren out of wedlock. She has since split up with this man and wants to have some "fun," so I have the two children most of the time.

We haven't seen our son in over a year. We're almost afraid to know what has happened to him. Our daughter is completely irresponsible. All of this has taken a terrible toll on my husband's health as well as my own. We are old before our time and sick at heart about how our lovely children have turned out. We feel guilty that we didn't do things right somehow, and then we just sink into a pit of anger and disappointment. I frequently sing a song called "A Very Special Grace," and through God's grace, we are surviving all the pain and loss. It's hard to love our children as we once did, and I feel guilty about that too.

A. You are learning firsthand the timeless truth that our faithful Lord is the only One we can count on. His love will sustain you and your husband through anything. He asks you to love your children unconditionally, just as He loves you. How, under these sad circumstances, can you do that? By continuing to pray for your children.

Miracles are wrought by prayer. Ruth Bell Graham prayed for her son, and the prodigal returned to take over the largest evangelistic association in the world for his father, Billy Graham. Countless other stories prove the power of prayer. Release your cares to the Lord regularly. He will take them from you. He has His hand on your wayward children. Leave them with Him, and concentrate on grandparenting the two innocent children. As you do that, be sure to take good care of yourself. It is easy to neglect good nutrition and exercise habits when wrestling with anxiety and disappointment.

There is always hope for grown children who have gone astray. Sometimes, only the Lord can bring the lamb back into the fold. Pray with thanksgiving that He is making it happen right now. Live each day not in sorrow but in the joy of the risen Lord and the blessings you see in your two grandchildren. They are your focus now. You did the best you could as a parent. Your children's choices are not your fault.

Love your children unconditionally through prayer. God will not give up on them.

Forgiving Adult Children

Q. My daughter is thirty-five, a drug addict, and has been unstable since she was fifteen. I have legal guardianship of her girls, ages ten and nine. I received them six years ago from an environment of filth and deprivation you wouldn't believe. I love my granddaughters, but my whole life has been turned upside down. I never dreamed my grandparenting years would be like this!

Sometimes I think it would be easier if she died. Then I could forget and heal. Instead, it never ends. She shows up and screams at the girls, "This woman is not your mother! Don't you ever forget who your real mother is!"

I have to confess to you, I have feelings of hate for my daughter. I'm not proud of it, but she has caused me so much pain.

A. It is time to forgive your daughter, not for her peace of mind, but for yours. Carrying hate is too heavy a burden. Hate is like acid. It eats away at your insides and then creeps into your relationships with others. Although hate is a normal reaction and one of which you should not feel ashamed, releasing the hate by forgiving will be a fresh, new beginning for you. What you call hate is really deep disappointment, grief, and loss.

Karen O'Connor in her book, *Restoring Relationships with Your Adult Child*, discusses the four stages of forgiveness. First you *hurt* with pain you don't deserve and can't forget. Then you *hate*, and that's where you are now. In this second stage of forgiveness, you "cannot shake the memory of how much you were hurt and cannot wish your enemy well."[1] In your case, the hurt is not over. It shows up, shaking up the status quo, and making it doubly hard for you to begin *healing*, which is the third stage of forgiveness.

Take action by seeing a qualified counselor who will work with you to forgive your daughter. Forgiveness can be accomplished in written form. That might be easier for you, since she is so distant and openly caustic. Do it by prayer if that is your only avenue, but do it!

Then see your attorney, who can initiate a restraining order to protect your granddaughters from unannounced and debilitating visits from their mother.

You will not forget what has happened, but, with professional help, you will heal. That will make the fourth stage of forgiveness a realistic possibility—*coming together*. It may take years. Coming together again in a peaceful, loving way with your daughter may never happen except in your own heart, after you have cleansed your heart of bitterness and have worked through the hurt.

Contact a counselor today to begin the process. Do not underestimate the power of forgiveness. We serve a miracle-making God.

The Consequences of Power Plays

Q. I would like to take my seven-year-old granddaughter to the mall and have her ears pierced. She begs me for it every time we're together. How can I convince my daughter-in-law that this is important to her child?

A. Don't touch this with a ten-foot pole! Your granddaughter begs you for pierced ears because her mother doesn't want it done, at least not yet. This is her mother's decision, and you must abide by it.

When the child begs, defer to the mother by saying that mother knows best. Assure your granddaughter that there will be time for such things later when she is older. Then, if and when mom gives in, you two can go to the mall for a special pair of earrings.

This is no different from any disagreement a grandmother has with a daughter-in-law such as using a pacifier, discipline matters, or access to the grandchildren. The parents are in charge of the children, and grandparents cannot use power plays to get accomplished what they believe should happen in the life of a grandchild.

Until mother gives the OK for pierced ears, show your love by listening and diverting your granddaughter's attention, and show your love and respect for your daughter-in-law by reinforcing her rules.

Grandparents Who Know Best

Q. Our grandson is fifteen and a straight-A student with a brilliant future, we are sure. His father passed away three years ago of heart failure, and we have been a strong emotional support to our grandson all of his life, but particularly during the last three years.

Our family has a history of West Point graduates: my father, my husband, and two uncles. We could assist our grandson in planning for his future schooling, but when we offered to do so, the boy refused to consider the military academy, saying he prefers to stay near home and attend a local school of small reputation. We think he feels that way now because he is young and will change his mind later. We think that his stepmother, our daughter, agrees with her son's choice, to ensure that he will be closer to her. We can understand that. However, the boy's future is at stake here. We don't think she is considering that. What shall we do?

A. How was your offer expressed? "This is what your grandfather and I think you should do" or "If you would like to consider West Point, Grandfather and I will be happy to assist you"? There's a *huge* difference between the two approaches, which could account for the rejection of your generous offer.

The cardinal rule for helpful grandparents is to have the best interest of the grandchild at heart. Your grandson's best interest may not be what you think. His dad died only three years ago. Your grandson still carries the loss every day, as do you, I'm sure. Your grandson's emotional safety net is his mother. It's natural and right that he would want to be close to her, and her concurrence with his wishes may be a combination of wanting (needing) him close by *plus* giving him the opportunity to make his own choices as he grows to manhood.

What *we* think cannot be thrust upon a grandchild. Fifteen is a very young age. Your grandson may change his mind. Until that time comes, continue your good work of supporting him and his mother with an understanding and loving heart. The continuation of a long-standing family tradition at West Point may yet be realized, if not by your grandson, perhaps one day by his son.

Partnering with Parents

Q. Recently, my seventeen-year-old granddaughter, who will start college in the fall, came to me needing $2,000 for a computer for school. She's a good kid, gets good grades, and has a part-time job to pay me back, so I gave it to her. I wrote her a check. Well, her mother (my daughter) is saying I shouldn't have done that. I can afford it, and she'll pay me back someday. Can't a grandfather do a good thing for his grandchild?

A. Certainly! Small things. But this is a *big* thing. This is a thing that required you to partner with your granddaughter's parents before even thinking about writing that check. One of the hardest issues for grandparents is control, especially when it comes to money. Loving, caring parents try to instill in their children the need for good planning for their future needs, saving money, taking responsibility and accountability for their spending. When a grandparent hands over money without consulting with parents, he creates an idea that money is easy to get—just ask Grandpa. This is naturally offensive to a parent and will cause a family feud such as you are experiencing.

Also, you probably will not get your money back. Most students entering college, part-time job or not, won't have an extra $2,000 to pay

Grandpa back, at least not for a long, long time. Did you write the loan down on paper? Have you set a time frame for her to pay you back? I suspect not.

Expressing your love by giving money with no accountability on the part of the child and no notification or partnering with her parents has you in the doghouse. Apologize to your daughter. She'll know you did this thing out of love. If you had talked with her about it before giving the money, none of this would have happened.

You can give away all the money you want; but when it's given to a seventeen-year-old grandchild, bringing mom and dad into the transaction before you give it is *crucial.*

DAUGHTERS AND DAUGHTERS-IN-LAW

The Special Mother-Daughter Bond

Q. I think my daughter and I are joined at the hip. She is thirty-four and the wonderful mother of two of our grandchildren. I can feel sick, and the phone will ring: "Hi, Mom. How are you feeling?" There are times when I can't get her off my mind, so I'll drive over to say hello, and, sure enough, she needs me. Since the hour she was born, I can't imagine life without her. I love her two brothers every bit as much, but there is something indescribable about the way I feel about my daughter and the way she feels about me. Do other mothers tell of this blessing?

A. Yes, indeed! The mother-daughter bond drives women to thoughts and actions that connect them in an unusual way. There is no doubt. Whether it is "I'm becoming my mother!" or "Somehow, I know she needs me," a mother and a daughter have a connection that defies description.

Enjoy it. Cherish this very special relationship secretly. Living as mother and daughter is richly rewarding and an honor to God.

Try not to make more of it than it really is, though. Remember, God made us of finer clay, not silly putty.

Mother! You're in Her Bones!

Q. I am a first-time grandparent-to-be; the baby is due in four months! I thought I knew my daughter until she became pregnant. We've always shared everything, well, almost everything. Now she tells me she doesn't want me at the hospital when my grandchild is born. She says she and my son-in-law will call me afterward! I'd at least like to know when she is in labor and going to the hospital. She insists on doing everything herself and is still going to her line-dancing classes each week.

I'm afraid she's got the same stubborn streak I exhibited when I was her age. I'm worried about her, and I'm worried about my grandchild. Can you help?

A. Judith Balswick quoted a line in her book, *Mothers and Daughters Making Peace,* that I'll never forget:

"Your mother is in your bones."

How true that is! In order to understand our daughters, especially pregnant ones, we need to understand ourselves and the imprint we have made on our girls. Balswick calls the mother-daughter relationship "the most intimate, tangled, beautiful and frustrating relationship shared by women."[2] I agree.

Most women see themselves in their daughters at one time or another. Usually, it is positive, sometimes it is not. The important thing is that we recognize that even though we may be alike in some ways, we are different in others. Once we acknowledge that, we can begin to relate to one another in positive ways.

Your daughter is sparring with you for control of her life. She's laying down rules of her choice, taking charge. I suggest that you become an active partner in her pregnancy by telling her just how much like you she is at this time in her life, then leaving the power struggle behind and concentrating on the joys that await you as a grandparent.

In four short months, you will have achieved something that, for most women, is a major life goal—you'll be a grandparent! This is just the warm-up! Wait patiently with love and understanding for the main event!

The Daughter I Thought I'd Never Have

Q. We have one child, our son, and I confess that I worried about the kind of girl he would marry. As it turned out, I couldn't have chosen a better wife for him than the one he has. She is everything I would want in a daughter. She loves the Lord, is kind, generous, and an excellent mother to our three grandchildren. She cooks dinner on Wednesday nights at church, makes meals fit for a king at home, and her cookies and cakes are legendary in our area. She sings and helps with the children's choir. She's smart as a whip about bargains and takes good care of the finances. I think my son got the Proverbs 31 woman, and I couldn't be happier.

I get great joy out of telling my granddaughter what a terrific mother she has. I only hope I can measure up as a grandmother.

A. You are truly blessed to have such a gifted daughter-in-law. Some grandparents tell me they walk softly around their daughters-in-law because their ideas and parenting styles are so opposite. Others say that no matter what they do, the relationship is strained, and there's little joy and friendship there.

So thank God for your gift, and don't worry about measuring up. I feel sure that your grandparenting style will add much to the family and enhance your relationship with your daughter-in-law as both of you strive to be the women God wants you to be.

The Nineties Parent

Q. Sometimes I can hardly believe my daughter is my daughter. She and I have such different ideas. I started noticing it most when she got married and became a mother. I always felt her opposition to my teaching would disappear then, but it has only intensified. If I didn't know better, I'd think she was trying to compete with me. The way she is raising our grandchildren is certainly not the way she was raised. We had rules. She has few. There was discipline in our house. She draws no lines, so the children do as they please. She says that it's the nineties and that I should adjust to the new styles of parenting.

I've always been open to good ideas, but the way things are, I don't feel I have much of a role as grandmother to the children, and I feel somewhat robbed. No, I *do* feel robbed.

How can a mother and daughter be so different?

A. Unfortunately, daughters don't grow *up "Guaranteed to operate according to instructions."* It's more like, *"Caution. Some parts have rough edges."*

Daughters with parenting ideas so different from yours can cramp your grandparenting style for sure. I am reminded of my Grandmother Burch who gave birth to seventeen, had fifty-nine grandchildren and forty-two greats. She used to say, "Be patient. Let Jesus do His work."

Patience is a great virtue in grandparenting. What worked for us years ago as a parent may be looked upon as old hat today. Hopefully our children will take what was good about their growing up and balance it with new ideas and methods. When they fail to do that, it is up to us to keep the lines of communication open, expressing feelings in a nonconfrontational and loving way. We also need to understand that we are not in control of our grandchildren. The parents are. We can teach and model for our grandchildren from our perspective by who we are and how we live. Do that, and your grandchildren will learn from you as well. When they grow up to become parents, they'll make their own decisions. That's the way it goes. We can never have it all our way.

Pray for and support your daughter. She loves you and undoubtedly falls back on your good training. She's exerting her independence and judgment, and she has every right to do that. Your open, honest, and unconditional love for her will keep you close, and your grandchildren will survive.

SONS AND SONS-IN-LAW

Two Sons as Different as Night and Day

Q. We have two sons, both grown. One finished college and has a good job and a nice family with two of our grandchildren, whom we love very much. Our second son also gave us a grandchild, a boy born to his girlfriend, who already had a daughter from her previous boyfriend. He and the mother did not get married because they really didn't even like each other; they liked to drink together.

Before this grandson was a year old, we had been asked to keep him for the summer, which turned into five years. We have decided he will be ours forever because our son has only come to visit three or four times. The mother is long gone, no one knows where.

We're glad to have our grandson safe and happy with us but feel sick at heart about the irresponsibility and choices of our second son. We wonder, *how in the world could our two sons be so different?*

A. Life choices are individual for each of us—mother, father, daughter, or son. Two sons raised in a good home, presented with the same set of values, the same loving care and encouragement, will do as they wish in adulthood. Choices might be exhibited in the form of rebellion, born perhaps of a secret jealousy of the older brother who has done so well or a nagging fear that he himself may not measure up. That is not to say parenting techniques were at fault. Parents can be part of the problem, but *we are not responsible for the choices of our grown children.*

The worst repercussion of your second son's life choices is that your grandson has suffered the loss of a secure home, a mother, and a fatherly influence. You and your husband are providing that, however, and I commend you for taking on such a tremendous responsibility.

You are saving a life. Concentrate on that job. You did your best with your two sons. Do your best for your grandson, and thank God you can be there for him.

Spiritual Headship of His Family

Q. Our great concern right now is for our daughter-in-law and grand-children because our son is not the spiritual head of the household. He coaches two different sports teams so that our daughter-in-law is the one to take the children to events at church. He's usually at a game on Family Night at the church. She shows up as a single mom every Wednesday. On Sundays, he rarely comes to church, preferring to sleep in or watch an important sports event on television. The grandchildren are ages five, six, and nine. Their mother has family devotions with them in the evening before bed.

Our son has always been strong willed, even as a child. We don't want to cause a fuss, but we don't like what we see nor the fact that our son is not living the faith he knows. The nine-year-old grandson is much like his father and is starting to balk at going to church, preferring to be with his dad, watching sports.

We are very close to our daughter-in-law. Is there anything my husband and I can do to change this situation before the example our son is setting causes real damage to his children and his marriage?

A. Which one of you is closest to your son, you or your husband? Whoever is closest to him needs to take him to breakfast or lunch and have a heart-to-heart. (Both of you going would show a united front but could be construed as "ganging up" on him.)

The Bible teaches loving confrontation. Your son needs to hear the truth from someone he trusts and admires. Strange as it may seem, sons with capable wives may not see or want to admit their wrongdoing as long as everybody's needs are being met.

Confront him with loving "I" statements: "I'm concerned for you and for your family." "I'm here to help." Make no accusatory "you" statements: "Do you know what you are doing to your family?" "You'd better get your spiritual life in order!"

Pray about it, and make the appointment only when you have peace that the time is right. Tread softly! Speaking out can be misconstrued as speaking out of turn. That will not be the result if one of you goes to your son having prayed beforehand. As a grandparent, loving confrontation is the right thing to do when the spiritual lives of grandchildren may be in jeopardy.

Once a parent, always a parent; some responsibilities remain. One of them is to warn of danger and to do it with a sweet spirit and a loving heart. Another is to remind children of scriptural truths. So, let's talk about your daughter-in-law for a moment. Since you are close to her, find a time to share with her this valuable reminder from writer Susan Raborn:

> What is the motivation behind wanting your spouse to love the Lord? Is it to have peace in the home instead of hostility? To raise up children in the will and admonition of the Lord? To have spiritual intimacy? To save your marriage? To be assured of your spouse's eternal destiny? These things are by no means improper goals, but concentrating on the problems distracts from our mission, which is to glorify God in any situation. By doing that, we will develop a deeper acceptance of His sovereignty, even if that means the spouse never accepts Christ.[3]

Begin a prayer partnership with your daughter-in-law, praising and thanking God for your son, her husband, and the father of your grandchildren. Thank God for the work He is doing in your son's life. Acknowledging with your daughter-in-law that God is the author and perfecter of our faith will give her an inner peace for this situation. Trust that God is working on it.

One other thought . . . save your money, and buy your son a VCR for his next birthday.

My Son-in-Law Isn't Working

Q. What can you do with a lazy, good-for-nothing son-in-law who won't lift a finger to provide for his family? Our daughter is working two jobs to support them and our grandson while this guy loafs around the house and makes halfhearted stabs at getting a job. My wife is over there all the time helping out. She takes his side to keep the peace, telling me this fellow is doing the best he can. Well, I don't buy it!

A. I don't buy it either. My concern is the poor example your son is setting for your grandson. Boys learn habits from Dad, both the good and the bad ones.

Since your wife is going over to help out, she is too close to the situation to change it. I'm afraid it's up to you, Dad.

First, you need to work on your attitude. It's natural to be upset about what's going on, but how you feel cannot be allowed to creep into the plan. The plan is this:

Invite your son-in-law over some evening soon. Tell him you care about him and that you're crazy about his wife and your grandson. You want to help him get a job. Have some coffee together while you explore with him three fields in which he would like to work. Then show him how to put together a good résumé and how to get ready for interviews. Stationery stores have résumé forms. Invest in a book that has interviewing tips and other helps you can look over together.

You get the picture . . . you become partners. There are manifold blessings to this relationship, for your grandson and his mother and then for your relationship with your son-in-law.

Hate what he has been doing, but don't hate him. He needs a plan. You can provide that and stand with him, man-to-man, until he succeeds.

Helping Your Adult Child Fail

Q. For the last three years since his divorce, I have done my best to stand by my son, who has visitation with his two children on Wednesday nights and every other weekend. He lost his job, so I set him up in an apartment with an extra bedroom for the kids and got him a phone. My husband hired him at the home business we have. He delivers parts to customers, driving my husband's truck.

He is constantly late to work but doesn't offer any apology. Even though we pay him generously for his skill level and the hours he puts in, it's never enough. I go over often, usually to help out with the kids, otherwise they wouldn't eat right.

I'm happy to do all this, but it doesn't seem to be helping. My friend says I am "enabling." I know what that means, but if I don't help him and the kids, who will?

A. *He* will! He's the only one who can break the pattern of irresponsibility and ingratitude, which probably was a factor in his divorce. You've paid for his home, given him a job, helped with the grandchildren, and by doing all of this good work, you have enabled your son to continue in an inconsiderate and negative pattern of failure.

Paying for the apartment and the phone relieved him of the responsibility. Giving him a job was a grand gesture he seems to flaunt in your face. Helping out for the children's sake is admirable except that you are doing their father's job.

Try some tough love: "I love you but, it's time you took charge of your life and your responsibilities. I can no longer help you financially. The children may have to spend more time with their mother. I'll be here to help you in any crisis, but I will not be coming over on a regular basis anymore."

Ask your husband to use the same tough love: "I'm glad to have you with the company, Son, but you'll have to be on time and show more interest or someone will take your place."

Then pray that your son takes control and begins a new pattern of honorable living—for his children's future and his own.

THE OTHER GRANDPARENTS

The In-Laws

Q. We have a situation in our family that is at the breaking point unless something is done about it. We have seven children, all grown, who have given us eight wonderful grandchildren. The problem is with the other set of grandparents of the twin boys that were born to our youngest daughter and her husband. They seem to compete with us for the affection and attention of the children. We had a friendly relationship with these folks for the first several years of our children's marriage. It's been cooling since the twins were born four years ago. Every birthday, Christmas, or any other holiday, these people lavish gifts on the twins. For example, I bought the twins matching teddy bears for their third birthday. The other bought *each one* an expensive motorized car that they won't be able to play with for at least a couple of years. Since they have a lot more money than we do, they take the boys on long trips, and they always come back loaded down with souvenirs and special clothing.

There are too many other instances like this to even tell you about all of them. My husband doesn't see that anything is wrong. He's just avoiding the issue.

I may have little money, but I've got a big mouth. After the last birthday incident, I called up this grandmother and read her the riot act. Now everybody's mad at me—my daughter, her husband, the other set of grandparents, and my husband, who thinks I overreacted. Did I overreact?

A. Maybe. You allowed yourself to feel pressured after four years of knowing you were going to be outdone no matter what you did for your twin grandsons. You cannot effect any change on the part of the other grandparent without damaging your relationship, but you can rethink your attitude toward what is going on.

Call and apologize nicely to the other grandmother. Tell her you were having a bad day, and do your best to get the relationship back on track for everyone's sake.

Remember this. Children are not dummies. They know who really loves them. They don't measure love by presents or money. We do! So, don't let it get to you. Continue to show your love for your twin grandsons from far and near. Do for them what you can do, the way you want to do it. They will love you no less.

Children can also be very clever about playing one grandparent against the other. If they see and feel what is going on, they may begin to play grandparent competition to the hilt if they can get away with it. All the more reason for you to be your loving, nonjudgmental self.

It takes two to make a quarrel. When one stops, there's no fight. Competition between sets of grandparents can cause bad feelings that reverberate throughout an entire family. Nip it in the bud now by changing *your* attitude, giving what you can with happiness in your heart, loving your twin grandsons so much they can't miss it, and being as pleasant as possible when you're around the other set of grandparents.

Sharing Holiday Time

Q. Almost every year, we have this unspoken hassle with our two daughters about whose house they'll be coming to for Christmas. Tension mounts as we near the date, and I know the other set of grandparents goes through the same thing. Nobody wants to hurt anybody's feelings, so we suffer in silence. Can you help?

A. There are two ways to solve this problem:

1. You be the set of grandparents that says, "Hey, kids, come for dinner if it works out that you can. You know we'd love to have you. If you don't make it, we're not going to love you any less. We respect your

choices and your feelings." That lets them off the hook completely. They make up their own minds freely, and you are not left wondering what plans to make.

2. Have a family meeting. Include the other grandparents and map out with a calendar who goes where and when. Then everybody knows, and there can't be any hurt feelings. Going to each grandparent's house every other year is a fine solution.

With our son's and daughter's families, it has worked well over the years to use the first option, adding, "If you go to their house, maybe you could drop by here for a piece of your favorite pie with us." If you are a very close and loving family, consider coming together for holiday events—both sets of grandparents and the whole family at one house. Maybe that's not possible every year, but occasionally.

It can't go on this way. Be the one to change it, lovingly, for everybody's sake. Then, peace on earth and goodwill toward men will truly reign in your family.

GREAT-GRANDPARENTING

It Just Gets Better!

Q. I had no idea anything could be better than being a grandparent until I became a great-grandparent! Watching my granddaughter go through her pregnancy with my daughter by my side has been one of the great joys of my life. Then, at the ripe old age of seventy-five, I was in the delivery room when my great-grandson was born! I cut the umbilical cord! Imagine!

He's two now, getting into everything just the way he should, and it's just such a privilege to go around after him and pick up. He calls me Ganny Nan, and he is the light of my life.

A. Amen from all great-grandparents everywhere! You are the same bright light to your grandson, Ganny Nan. Great-grandparents are treasured by children. One great-grandson speaks of his great-grandfather this way:

"Why, it's Gramps' presence alone that gives meaning to all of us. Through him we see each other. The man has thirty-five grandchildren and fifteen of us greats. He is the star attraction of the family! He told me once he had so many kids he ran out of names for them so he called them Brocade, Avalon, Channel, Newrail, and Oleomargarine. He said his wife wouldn't hear of that and gave them all Christian names. He called his twenty-first grandchild by the name of twenty-one, saying it was easier to remember that way."

Another young granddaughter says this about her great-grandmother:

"I visit my Nanny with my Grandma. Nanny is Grandma's mother. Boy, she is old! But she says she was like me when she was a little girl. I'm proud of that because I love her very much. She has things in my family that go back hundreds of years. I hope I can live as long as her. She's wonderful!"

More than 40 percent of today's senior citizens live to become great-grandparents, and there'll be more and more in the future as we are living longer, healthier lives. Great-grandparents symbolize family continuity and family history. Continue to wear your badge of honor with joy as does this eighty-two-year-old grandfather who lives with his granddaughter's family and is able to baby-sit his great-grandchildren. He wrote: "It's a new lease on life for me. They asked me to move in. I needed them, and they needed me! The kids are great. They listen to me when I tell them something, and we have a ball—that is, until their parents come home."

GREAT-GRANDMOTHER

I took a swallow from my cup
and watched the daughter of my grand
bound out the door to the school bus stop.

Her mother chattered with her mother.
There we were in the kitchen, mothers all.
Now four generations alive.

How sweetly odd to see these women
loving, sharing, laughing—grandmother,
granddaughter, and the great one out the door.

Odd because so short a while ago,
it was I who laughed with my mother,
I who bounded out the door.

Now, clutching tight my cup, matriarch of all,
I am overwhelmed by God's grace,
But where, oh where, did the time go?

HEROES

My Husband, the Hero

Q. My husband has always been a hero to me, but it really is fun to watch him with the grandchildren and see how they feel about him. Our thirteen-year-old grandson would rather listen to his grandfather tell stories about the old days than play on the computer! My husband has a way of making stories so exciting, so spellbinding, that the children are glued to every word. He tells them stories about his youth and his military service. Sometimes, the details vary, and I suppose the truth is stretched here and there, but that doesn't matter.

To our grandchildren, he's better than a sports star, a movie star, or the president. He is always ready to go somewhere, fix something, listen, or just plain relax with a grandchild who needs somebody to listen in the hammock in the yard. It's not unusual for grandfather and grandchild to fall asleep out there.

My hero husband has been especially important to our grandson who just turned seventeen and has had quite a few disappointments in his young life.

I guess you might say he is a hero to all of us, and we just thank God for him. Thanks for this chance to honor him.

A.   Congratulate your husband for me. I'm sure he'd agree that it doesn't take a lot to be a hero to children, and a grandfather is ideal for the job.

Vicki Elaine Legg, a writer from Petersburg, Indiana, expressed the effect a grandfather's stories can have on a young person:

> "Grandpa, remember that story about Gil Hodges and the curve ball?"
>
> He nodded then, and his face glowed with the pleasure of a happy memory. "Gil Hodges. Now there was a real American sports hero. Why, he hit four homers in one game at Ebbets Field against the Philadelphia Braves in August of 1950."
>
> I smiled and relaxed, hearing the familiar creak of the porch swing chains and Grandpa's voice as he told the story I had heard at least 100 times before.[4]

The ability to cause a grandchild to smile and relax with his stories also gives grandfather a platform from which to pass on values and Christian principles, richly sprinkled with his own personality and wit.

All are invited to be a hero to a child. Uncles, aunts, cousins, nieces, nephews, sisters, brothers—you're all welcome. Children need authentic heroes instead of overpaid athletes, disreputable movie stars, and other media pretenders who would purchase their temporary adoration.

Dealing with Change

Endurance is the ability to stand up under adversity;
perseverance is the ability to progress in spite of it.

JERRY BRIDGES[1]

Some children and grandchildren move away. So do grandparents. When children take their children far away from us, we miss them all so very much and search for ways to stay in touch. How to cope with the loss of a nearby relationship with grandchildren and how to keep the loving link from long distance are some of the often asked questions contained in section 6.

Another change with far more serious ramifications is the biggest problem facing Christian grandparents today—the divorce of an adult child, the parent of our grandchild(ren). Dealing with the pain, loss, and the complex emotional stresses brought onto the small shoulders of grandchildren is a burden only the Lord can lift. What is our role during the fray? Then, when the storm is over, and the landscape is littered with damaged, confused children of all ages, what can we do to effect a renewed hope for those we love and for ourselves?

Should an adult child with children go home again? And the remarriage of an adult child with children presents a whole new set of questions and prayer concerns.

Questions in this section also address the sticky issue of grandmother and grandfather splitting up and then remarrying.

As we live our long lives, we learn time and time again that we can count on change. Thanks be to God that He does not!

LONG-DISTANCE GRANDPARENTING

When They Move Away

Q. We have a good relationship with the grandchildren who live nearby, but we have two who live far from us. What are some ways to establish closer bonds with them? One is six, and the other is just starting high school.

A. Change is inevitable, and children move away, leaving us missing them and our grandchildren. Sometimes, we are the ones who move away from them. Here are sixteen ideas for you that go beyond just running up the phone bill:

1. Go ahead and call once a week, but be sure you know your grandchild's interests and activities, and talk about them when you phone. Initiate conversation by telling about something that happened to you, avoiding meaningless talk. Don't always fill the air with your voice. Wait patiently for answers and thoughts as youngsters take time to formulate what they want to say. Silence can be golden on the telephone as you hear with your own ears the wonderful words yours might have trampled on.
2. Your six-year-old will love an audio- or videotape of you reading a bedtime story. Mail the tape *and* the book. Ask the parent to videotape your grandchild watching you read and send that to you.
3. Cut out comic strips. Cover the words with whiteout, and write in your own. Mail them to your grandchild.

4. Pre-address envelopes. Write and mail notes on sacks, napkins, church bulletins, or whatever is available wherever you are and whenever you think of your grandchild.

5. Send inexpensive gifts on a day other than a birthday or holiday. Send a bookmark or stickers—a little something that says, "I love you." Posters are a hit and are easily mailed in cardboard tubes.

6. As your grandchild learns to read, write an original story of three or four paragraphs, glue it to colored paper, and mail it. Children love to receive mail addressed to them.

7. Take your grandchild's address with you when you travel. Buy a postcard from that area, address it, and write, "I saw this today and thought of you."

8. Keep a scrapbook of pictures of events you can show your grandchild the next time you get together.

9. Write letters about things that happen at your house: squirrels stashing their food under the tree stump, raccoons thumping onto the roof, birds singing in the feeder, your memories of your own childhood, and exciting events coming up. Ask questions in your letters that require a simple answer, and enclose self-addressed stamped envelopes to make it easier for the child to respond. Buy stationery with bright colors, so the child will recognize that it's a letter from you.

10. Send audiotapes of what happens at your house. Listening to the tapes makes the child feel part of your everyday life. Tapes with exclamations of love for the child will reinforce feelings for you.

11. If you and your grandchild have a computer, install E-mail, and you can talk to each other every day!

12. Plan a trip to see your grandchildren, or plan to bring them to you. Let your grandchildren be part of the planning by phone or by mail, adding to the excitement and anticipation.

13. Know what interests your high schoolers. If it's sports, be current on their favorite teams, or root for them when they play.

14. Friends are important to teens. Find out where your grandchildren hang out and with whom. Ask informed questions that show you are interested and concerned. Avoid unsolicited advice.

15. Food and music are other favorite teen topics. Send tapes they would like, approved by the parents. Mail favorite cookies or candies overnight. Share recipes and cooking tips.

16. Weave your faith into letters and phone calls. At some point, every child will doubt what they believe. You can be a stabilizing influence for your grandchild, someone to come to with serious questions or a need for encouragement.

One of my favorite long-distance grandparenting success stories was written by a grandmother from Syracuse, New York. Her infant granddaughter lived with her parents overseas. The grandmother prayed that somehow her granddaughter would understand that she loves her. She started adding a big red heart to the outside of specially written letters to the granddaughter. That went on for four years until the girl arrived at the airport, home at last! Grandmother was there to greet the shy little girl, who hid her face in her mother's pant leg. That is, until Grandmother held up a familiar envelope with a big red heart on it and opened her arms wide. She got a big warm hug. Love had crossed the ocean.[2]

YOUR CHILD'S DIVORCE

Taking Sides

Q. Our son-in-law and daughter started having problems over a year ago. It all began when his job changed and required a lot of travel. He didn't keep in good touch with his family, saying he was busy in late meetings. It turned out that he had an affair, and my daughter hit the roof and separated from him.

He tried to reach her by calling us, and I hung up on him. I called him names and told him I never wanted to see him again as long as I live for what he did to my daughter.

Well, they went to a Christian counselor and worked it out. They are back together now, and he doesn't want anything to do with me. I can't blame him, the way I treated him, but my daughter was so hurt. The worst part of all of this is that my time with my two adorable grandchildren has been restricted. Is there anything I can do to make it right, or is it too late?

A. It's never too late to make amends. It may take a while for him to accept your apology, but, for your sake first, you need to make it.

Write him a note and mail it, asking him to meet you somewhere to talk. When he comes, keep your apology brief. Don't go into details that might cause his memory to flare up. Hopefully, he will apologize to you for causing the family such pain, but he very well may not. You see, this is not your problem. This is something that happened to *his* family unit. Yes, it had a domino effect down into the entire family, but it was *their* problem to work out. I'm sure you see now, that taking sides during the separation was not your place. Your job was to stay neutral, pray for reconciliation, and keep an arms length away from controversy while they worked it out. And remember, your grandchildren love both parents, no matter what they do. Assure your daughter, in a private moment, that you will not speak against your son-in-law, so she will trust you with the children again.

Pending divorce is an emotional roller coaster for everybody. Grandparents are not the engineers and must stay in neutral gear for a smooth ride.

Answering Tough Questions

Q. My daughter has separated from her husband, and they are planning to divorce. I'm very close to my eight-year-old grandson. He spends a lot of time at our house, and I expect he'll be over even more now, since my daughter retains custody. I want to say the right things to him regarding the divorce. I'm going to try not to say anything bad about his father, even though the circumstances of the separation were his fault. I know my grandson is going to ask me to explain some things he's confused about. He's already started asking. What kinds of questions can I expect, and what's the best way to answer them?

A.   Your grandson is going to wonder who will take care of him, will he see his dad again, will there be enough money now, will he have to move and change schools, will Mom marry somebody else, will they keep him, and whether the whole thing his fault.

Your best answers will be reinforcing, encouraging, loving, and brief. Listen to him. Say little. Put yourself in his place. His perception of things will be very different from yours. Have fun with him, and hug him a lot.

You're doing a good job of staying out of the blaming department. Keep that up. Even if the separation was the fault of your son-in-law, he's still your grandson's father. There will be an ongoing relationship there. If the blame you feel gets into conversation with your grandson, however unintentionally, you will be contributing to further erosion of the child's confidence in his dad. Remember that in divorce, the child stands between two people he loves with all of his heart. It doesn't matter what either of them has done. He loves them both.

Coping with the Divorce of Your Child

Q.   We are living through the ramifications of our son and daughter-in-law's divorce, trying to do all the right things for our precious grandson and his two sisters. It's a long story of cheating and financial ruin, and it will take years for our son to regain his confidence and have peace about his future. Right now he is fighting for custody of his son, who is nine.

Our daughter-in-law has turned on all of us, is vindictive because she is in denial of her part in the divorce, and bars us from seeing the children as best she can. It's been a terrible struggle for my husband and me as we watch our grandchildren used as tools between the two parents. We mourn the loss of a daughter-in-law we had for twelve years, and we live with a lot of regret and guilt that we didn't see the signs of trouble. Maybe we could have helped. We wonder, will it ever be over?

A.   Divorce can seem worse than death because the person is still alive. You lose them, but they're still there, and the pain and loss persists like a bleeding wound that can't heal because it isn't closed. Divorce is difficult for grandparents because we grieve not only for our children but for our grandchildren, whose lives have been cracked at the foundation, leaving them unstable and unsure.

Continue doing all of the "right things." Some of those include:

- Let the parents focus on their troubles. You focus on the grandchildren.
- Pray daily for reconciliation of the young family and for God's protection of the children.
- Listen to the grandchildren when you are with them. Allow them to talk with little or no feedback from you. Keep your opinions to yourself in their presence, for they see the divorce from a different perspective, and they love both parents.
- Assure the children of your love often.
- Keep your normal schedule. Represent stability in their rocky world.
- Play with the children. Have fun together.
- Take care of your health. Body defenses break down without proper nutrition, rest, exercise, and relaxation.
- Be available as counsel to your son without injecting your ideas. Allow him to remain as the authority figure in your grandchildren's lives. Encourage him as he works to make a new life.
- According to Proverbs 10:12, when couples divide, let your love multiply.
- Remember, you are not responsible for the choices of your adult children.

FACTS

- In 1993 there were 1.2 million divorces in the U.S. Half of all divorcing couples had at least one minor child.
- Twenty-nine percent of all minors live in a single-parent home, a total of 17.3 million children.
- Each year an additional one million children experience the divorce or separation of their biological parents.
- Current divorce rates indicate that about 40 percent of children born to married mothers will experience the divorce of their parents.[3]

YOUR CHILD'S REMARRIAGE

Ask Questions before Remarriage

Q. We got the news last week that our daughter is going to remarry. She's only been divorced seven months and has had a hard time financially. She doesn't work. Our grandson, age three, has been hospitalized a number of times for chronic asthma, and because of his mother's shiftless first husband, there is no insurance. My husband and I have helped them with money quite a lot.

We don't know this new fellow at all; we've never met him. She hasn't been going with him long. Our oldest son was the one who told us about the marriage. I'm sure our daughter will bring him over. I just hope it's before the wedding so I can check him out. The last thing we would want to see is our daughter walking into a bad second marriage after the first one. How far should I stick my nose in here?

A. Definitely do your best to meet him before the wedding. If you can accomplish that, ask him questions in a nice way: "Tell me about your folks." "Are you making a career out of your current job?" You can't tell a book by its cover, but you can tell a lot about a prospective son-in-law by how he answers important questions and from his general demeanor.

With consistently more than three million reports of child abuse in America each year, grandparents wisely ask questions of men who would be step-parents to our grandchildren. Ask prudent questions of him in a caring, sincere way that will give you peace about the kind of parent he will be. Query such topics as whether his work is stable or whether he has good long-term goals, how he gets along with your grandchild, and whether he plans to nurture your grandchild's Christian faith. Then watch his body language. You can tell. You'll get a feeling.

Give your daughter a copy of Bobb and Cheryl Biehl's book, *Pre-Remarriage Questions* in the *Heart to Heart* series (Broadman and Holman). This book will help your daughter and her fiancé work through trouble spots before they marry.

If meeting him before the wedding is not possible, ask the questions of your daughter. If nothing else, you will make her think. She may be head over heels in love and ignoring some character flaws that could prove disastrous. Don't *tell* her what to think. *Make* her think. Let her come to her own conclusions.

Now, this fellow may be Prince Charming and the best thing that could have happened in your daughter's life, especially after her battle for financial independence. He may be the loving daddy you hoped for for your grandson. But you have a moral right to ask questions before the fact in a dignified, impartial way, for the sake of your daughter, her son, and their secure future. Just make sure you don't cross that fine line from genuine concern into meddling.

Money Isn't Everything

Q. We're happy that our divorced daughter is about to remarry. We've been supporting her and the two grandchildren for three years, and they have wanted for nothing.

The newly proposed head of this household obviously loves our daughter. The children seem to have bonded with him well. Our concern is whether or not this nice young man can take proper care of the family financially. He doesn't make much money, and the children are accustomed to having everything they need.

What can we do to ensure our grandchildren's financial security?

A.   Well done! You've stepped in as grandparents do, on an interim basis. Now, it's time to step aside, and let this new family make a life together.

Your daughter has a second chance at happiness, and your grandchildren will have a sense of security they haven't felt in years. Rejoice for them and for yourself. Having "enough" money is not important now to this new family. They have each other and a whole new life. The financial details of that new life are their business and not yours.

Be there for them, not with money in your hand, but with moral support, love, and a great big smile on your face. They still need you, but now you can just be a grandparent.

How Your Relationship Will Change

Q.   My son is remarried to a nice girl with one child of her own to add to his two. My grandchildren's mother has primary custody, but the kids spend a lot of time with their dad and his new wife.

During the two years my son was divorced and alone, I spent a lot of time at his house. I would clean for him, make dinner, and sometimes help the kids clean up so they could have more time together before they went back to their mother's. In the short time since the wedding, I haven't been invited over, they don't call, and I'm shy to call them for fear I'll be intruding. Is this normal? Am I just making a mountain out of a molehill and feeling hurt for no reason?

A.   It is perfectly normal that a newly married couple wants to be left alone for a while, particularly this one, with blending going on between his and hers.

You're a good mom and a good friend to your son, and I'm sure you are a loving grandmother. Give them time. Keep a happy spirit about this new family. Be glad they have found each other, and be ready in case they need you. As time goes by, you may indeed find that you are outside the circle of your son's married life. That's where grandparents live—on the edge, so to speak. We're not in charge anymore since our adult child has created his own family unit.

On the other hand, it may turn out that you are needed more than ever to be integrally involved in their lives. Whatever the case, pray for the family, thank God your grandchildren have a more stable environment in which to grow, and know that, without a doubt, the way you respond to the new marriage will make the difference in your relationship with your son and his family.

BRINGING CHILDREN BACK HOME

Should We Take Them In?

Q. What do you think about grown kids moving back into the house after a divorce? We're worried about what will happen to our daughter and granddaughter following a bitter divorce that will be final soon. I know our daughter will have a rough time making ends meet. She hasn't said anything to us yet, but I think she might. How should I respond, and if she doesn't ask us, should we offer our home?

A. Countless grandparents ask this question as the divorce rate, though it has leveled off in the last decade, remains high with one of every two first marriages failing.

I advocate the three "Ps" if you're thinking about bringing them back home: *Pray*, make a *plan*, and *partner* with your child. The plan is important if you decide to do this, because if all you do is open your arms and your front door, without a few rules and regulations, you risk becoming parent to everybody.

Your plan might include length of stay, amount of rent, transportation and housework details, who buys and cooks the food, discipline of your grandchild while under your roof, and house rules for watching television and when the lights go off. When these issues are discussed lovingly before your child and grandchild move in, everybody knows what is expected, and there will be fewer problems.

If your daughter is hesitant to ask you about moving back, and you sense that, have a talk with her about future plans. Let her know you are interested in her welfare and your grandchild's future and are there to help if she needs you.

Honoring Your Children's Choices

Q. My older daughter thinks I am meddling because I very much want my young son to come back home. He has custody of my only grandchild, a sweet one-year-old boy, and it makes good sense to me because I can take care of him during the day. What better place for him than at his grandmother's?

My son refuses to move in, and I just don't understand it. He's got a small apartment and takes the baby to day care when he could be here safe and sound. Everybody's mad at me, but all I want to do is make things easier for him.

A. The way to make things easier for your son is to give up the thought that he and the baby will come live with you. It may seem right to you, but, obviously, your son, for whatever reason(s) disagrees. Maybe he feels he has something to prove. He wants to do this on his own. Perhaps your personalities would clash under the same roof because his ideas for his future or his son's future are different from yours. What reasons has he given you? Accept those reasons, and be available in a pinch.

After some time has gone by and everybody settles into a routine, ask your son if he'd like you to baby-sit two days a week. That would save some day-care expense and give you time with your grandchild.

Grandparent maturity requires that we allow our adult children to make their own decisions about their welfare and that of their children. Work on making yourself so agreeable that your son can't resist you.

Don't build a wall. Carefully and lovingly build a bridge.

YOUR DIVORCE, YOUR REMARRIAGE

When Grandma and Grandpa Split Up

Q. My wife and I have been married thirty-six years. We have four successful children and seven beautiful grandchildren. I thought we would grow old together, but my wife has decided she wants to find out what to do with the rest of her life and wants a divorce. She says she wants to travel, which I don't like to do, and she says she's bored. I don't think there's another man or anything like that, but she's sure of what she wants to do and says she wants me to talk to the kids.

I've talked to our pastor and, pretty soon, I'll have to let the family know. I'll have to wait until my own feelings subside. Frankly, I don't know how to feel. I'm numb. How do I break this to my kids?

A. Divorce at any age hurts. A shock like this hits hard, and it will also be hard for your family to hear.

Enlist the partnership of your pastor to tell the kids. Depending on your personal closeness with your grown children, go to the one or ones you are most comfortable with and break the news gently and without bitterness.

The news will filter down to the grandchildren, who will need to spend time with you. Their emotions will run the gamut of shock, disbelief, anger, sadness, and a feeling of loss to wanting to make it go away. They won't understand the details, so don't belabor them. Grandma will still be a part of their lives. Help the children understand she is leaving you, not them.

It's a shame you have to be the one to tell. The two of you should do this together.

Be philosophical, reassuring, and nonjudgmental as you tend to this task. And spend time on your knees in prayer. Women have been known to change their minds. God, who can make flowers grow from stone and the desert bloom like a rose, can also restore your broken marriage if it is His will in your life. Ask Him how you can help.

Grandparents Marrying Again

Q. I'm seventy-one and have been divorced for twenty years. My former husband and I had two fine children, and I have been quite close to them and content with my life. One of my adult children counts on me in a number of ways, and I have enjoyed the strong bond I have with that family.

I have received a proposal of marriage from a fine, upstanding man who is a recent widower with no children. He is pleased at the prospect of acquiring ready-made grandchildren. He goes to my church, and we have been attending events together for some time because we have similar interests. We have fun, and I have accepted his proposal and am quite excited about the whole thing.

The trouble is, my two children and their families are going to be surprised, I think. I have often said I would not marry again, but I didn't expect to fall in love again. This is the right thing for me to do. How do I convince them of that fact?

A. No convincing necessary. Just tell them. They'll probably be delighted for you. Assure both of your children that you will remain active in their lives and that you look forward to introducing your intended to them. Bring him along on the second visit. Having him with you as you break the news will be too intimidating for the children, and they may hold back feelings.

I am happy for you both and wish you a long and loving life together. You'll be fine. Your situation is not as complicated as when some grandparents remarry and the circumstances surrounding the new marriage result in hostility and even disconnection from the family. Bitter power struggles over grandchildren and step-grandchildren happen, and sometimes the adult child who strongly objects to the new marriage never accepts the step-grandparent at all.

These sad stories usually stem from bad choices on the part of grandparents who move in with someone before marriage, are perceived by their children to have moved too quickly into marriage following divorce without preparing the family, or are seen spending lavishly both their time and money in a relationship that the children think probably won't last.

It's not easy. Grandparents considering a new marriage should keep in mind that your loved ones will need to see that your choices continue to reflect the Christian values you have always exhibited and taught to them.

Happy Times

LOVE AND LAUGHTER

READING AND STORYTELLING

HAVING FUN

SURROGATE GRANDPARENTING

Happy Times

Grandchildren need to play.
We are blessed when they want to play with us.

LOVE IS THE FOUNDATION FOR HAPPY TIMES with grandchildren. Because we grandparents love our grandchildren unconditionally, we do the unexpected, go the extra mile, ignore their missteps, encourage new beginnings, and bring a measure of joy and laughter into their lives.

Happy times are the stuff of which memories are made. Quiet, happy times, like reading a book with a grandchild or telling a favorite story, walking and talking together or cuddling on the couch, can leave an indelible imprint on the lives of children who, because a grandparent found time to be with them, knew they were loved.

The questions in section 7 are all about love and laughter, spending time and playing with our grandchildren.

LOVE IN ACTION

The grandfather who works all day and night to make his grandchild's bike like new.

The grandmother who goes to summer camp with her grandchild.

The grandfather who teaches his grandson the difference between needing something and wanting it.

Grandparents who surprise an accomplished grandchild with a dress-up appreciation dinner.

The grandmother who buys the supplies, then shows a grandchild how to make her own Christmas gifts.

LOVE AND LAUGHTER

Grandmother's Old Apron

Q. My mother passed away two years ago. We missed her terribly at my daughter's wedding last July. The two of them were especially close. For twenty years, they shared a love that was obvious to our entire family, a special relationship that enhanced both of their lives. I know my mother relished every moment with her granddaughter. She taught her so many things, like how to can fruits and vegetables, to make pickles, and all according to her tried-and-true recipes from years back. Mother always wore the same apron, yellow, quite faded now, with a ruffle around the edge and two large pockets in front. Those pockets variously held our daughter's baby bottles, teething ring, unusual living and dead creatures from her backyard received as gifts from her granddaughter, small school pictures, a tear-soaked handkerchief when our daughter was sick, and any number of small mementos from the years of her granddaughter's growing up.

This was the apron mother held up to her face to play hide and seek, to wrap her granddaughter in to protect her against a breeze, her uniform of love for their joyous work together in her kitchen for all those years.

Knowing what it would mean to our daughter, I put that old apron of mother's in a silver box, wrapped it with gold ribbon, and gave it to her as a wedding present. She was overcome with tears of joy, and I know she will treasure this tangible memory of her grandmother's love. I hope she will pass it on to her own daughter one day as a symbol of her love and devotion.

A.   Thank you for your touching letter. Aprons hold a special significance in the lives of many mothers, daughters, and granddaughters. One grandmother made a fine quilt for her granddaughter who was to be married. Each square represented a year of the girl's life up to the date of her marriage, and in the center of the quilt, the grandmother had sewn a four-inch piece of one tie from the apron she had worn for years because it was a favorite of her granddaughter.

In the card that went with the gift, the grandmother wrote about the meaning of the center of the quilt, calling it, "the tie that binds us together in love."

Unconditional Grandparent Love

Q.   We have four grandchildren, three girls and a boy. We have always loved them and have done our best to show that. One of the children, the boy, has never warmed up to us. He is eighteen now and still distant. It is a real disappointment to us, but mostly to my husband, who has done his level best to give of himself and his time and ideas for all these years to no avail. The boy is popular, bright, and goes with a good crowd of friends. He's not a bad kid. I think he just doesn't like us.

His sisters have always shown us respect and courtesy, even love and hugs, which are wonderful; however, we think we'd better give up on the boy. We've done about all we can, unless you have a suggestion.

A.   Yes, I do. Do not give up on your grandson. Grandparent love is not measured in the return of that love but by its unconditional quality and surety.

Continue to pray for and love this distant grandson. He's still maturing. One day, all you have done and said, all the love you have exhibited in his life, will bear fruit. When the major events of his life take place—

graduation, marriage, and parenthood—you will probably see a new attitude, borne of experience and maturity.

Be patient and love him without expecting anything back. It will come. If he does not demonstrate it as the years go by, still do not give up on him.

God's love has no boundaries. Neither does it cease, as we read in *The Blessing of His Love* by Charles H. Spurgeon:

> There is a fragrance in His perfume that only His heart could produce. There is a sweetness in His honeycomb that has the very essence of His soul's affection mingled with it. May we continually taste and know the blessing of His love.[1]

God's way is to offer love forever with the hope that it will be understood and acknowledged. Let that be your way also.

Grandchildren Are Just Plain Fun!

Q. Since our grandchildren came along, I didn't know how much fun my husband could be with kids. I've never heard him laugh so much in my life.

We have pigs and chickens, and he likes to teach the kids about them. He has amazed me with a newfound sense of humor and a zest for living when the grandkids are around. He figures out new ways to entertain them and places to take them and, of course, they just love it. They go to the fairs, and there's a big tractor parade they wouldn't miss each summer.

I asked him about this one day, and he said he just feels so relaxed with them. He knows they will go home with their parents, and he gets to enjoy them without all the stress he felt when our son was growing up.

It just thrills me to see how much fun my husband is getting out of grandparenting.

A. My mother, grandmother of twenty-eight, used to say, "I love to see the children come, and I love to see them go." She meant no disrespect in that remark. There were just times when she had had enough fun. Honest grandparents admit to this feeling, and it is legitimate.

With all of the responsibilities the job carries, grandparenting is still basically fun. God wants us to have fun. We know that laughter, too, is good medicine that can actually keep grandparents healthier.

I'm very happy for both of you and hope that you, Grandmother, are having every bit as much fun with those grandchildren as your husband!

Laughter Is Good Medicine

Q. I'm a new grandmother. My only grandmother passed away when I was ten. She was a Christian, and I'm sure she had many fine qualities, but all I really remember about her is that she was not a happy person. I don't plan to repeat that role model with my grandchildren. I think laughing and having a playful attitude are important for children. I made a point of having fun with my own, and I think it made a real difference in their attitude toward life now that they are grown.

It's the little things that count, and I think we should have a good laugh about *something* every day. I wonder what you think about that.

A. You're absolutely right. Being around grumpy grandparents can stunt your growth. A parent once told me that taking her children to see Grandma became prohibitive because, each time, the grandmother would gather the children to her, close her eyes, and begin a litany of all that was wrong, ending with a plea to go be with Jesus. Soon the children didn't want to visit anymore because Grandma wasn't happy about anything despite all their efforts to bring her joy. Parents, too, shy away from exposing children to such a negative example.

If a grandchild is asked to rate the best thing about coming over to your house, you want him or her to say, "Because we have so much fun." Laughter is a big part of having fun.

We owe it to our grandchildren to see the humor in life. At their home, the demands are great: "Clean your room." "Be in by ten." "Eat that spinach." "Do your homework." Bringing a little laughter into life is a welcome relief from the inevitable heavy loads they carry every day at school, at home, and at work. It keeps everybody sane, more relaxed, and is a vital tool for getting through difficulties, pressures, and losses.

Comedian Bill Cosby has said, "Once you find laughter, no matter how painful your situation might be, you can survive it."

Laughter has even been found by scientists to release natural painkillers into the body that combat arthritis and reduce the number of stress-producing hormones.

Laughter can even turn what seems to be a dire situation into a hilarious one if somebody has a sense of humor. One grandma got all gussied up for a special event, and as she and her husband walked along a sidewalk to the car, a sprinkler hose on the grass burst, drenching her, her fancy dress, and her hairdo. Grandpa had his camera handy, got the picture, and mailed it to their long-distance grandchildren!

Laugh for your grandchildren until it's infectious. Teach them that life with Jesus Christ is *full* of joy.

> A keen sense of humor helps us
> to overlook the unbecoming,
> understand the unconventional, tolerate the unpleasant,
> overcome the unexpected, and outlast the unbearable.
> Billy Graham[2]

READING AND STORYTELLING

Encouraging a Love for Books

Q. I inherited a love of reading from grandparents who made a point of having books available for me to read every time I visited. My grandparents did not own a television set. I spent a lot of time at their house during my elementary and high school years and never missed TV because the bookcase was always there by the couch. I could choose any book I wanted and could lose myself in the adventures of timeless books with life lessons that, I'm sure, have affected who I am today.

Do you have any tips for helping our little grandchildren, who are now seven and eight, to develop a love of reading books? This habit, however well taught to him, seems to have escaped their father, our son, who has always had a love affair with TV and videos.

A. Your own grandparents had a good idea, placing the bookcase in clear view. I have done that for my grandchildren. Like your son, though, most of ours opt for the television set that sits there as well.

The idea of videos is a good one. There are free videos at your local library that will help grandchildren learn which books to read according to their interests. Videos of well-known books encourage young children to want to read those books for themselves, especially if they know a loving grandparent might read it with them.

Your two grandchildren are coming to the perfect age for instilling this good habit that, as you have learned, can affect their lives in a positive way. When you have them with you, go to the library. Teach them how to use the library, to be comfortable with it, to respect the peace and quiet there, and to make good choices of books for their reading level.

Become known in your family as the grandparent who takes the children to the library. It will be a habit for which they will thank you the rest of their lives.

Reading and Telling Stories

Q. Our three-year-old grandson likes nothing better than to curl up in my lap to hear a story. I've never felt that I was very good at it, but he gets such joy from it, I find myself thinking up new ideas for stories for him. Any ideas for me?

A. Reading aloud and storytelling are real bonding experiences for grandparent and child. One idea for you is to read a lot yourself and select those books you know would be exciting or interesting to your grandson, then tell him a story from them. Then, as your grandchild grows older, introduce him to the books with which he is now familiar because of your stories!

Tell him stories from the Bible. Tell stories of missionaries and other great people from Christian history. Make up poems and teach them to him, poems with lessons of friendship, sharing, and caring. Animal stories are always a hit with small grandchildren. Let your storytelling leave the child with one small lesson learned.

For one of my granddaughters, I write brief, original stories with three purposes: 1) to glorify God, 2) to teach the value of friendships, and 3) to present to the child one new word she did not know before, a word she has to ask about or look up.

Congratulations on your initiative and for being so generous with your time and love. You know there is no sweeter sound than a grandchild purring, "Grandma, tell me a story?"

HAVING FUN

Keeping Grandchildren Happy

Q. We will have two grandchildren, ages seven and twelve, for a month this summer while their parents are away on a buying trip for their business. We love these children very much and look forward to having them all to ourselves. My husband and I are in our mid-sixties and in good health, but it has been a while since we had kids in the house for that length of time.

Any suggestions on how we can keep them happy?

A. Good, you're planning ahead! A child of any age will want to play and have fun—all the time if they can get away with it. That doesn't necessarily mean it will be expensive or wear you out.

If grandchildren came with a handbook informing us of their needs, *play* would be at the top of the list along with *love*. In fact, playing with grandchildren is a form of loving them. Every child needs to play, and we are blessed when they want to play with us!

You have a close relationship, so you probably know what interests them. If not, ask the parents. Build your plan for the month around those interests. For example, if it's sports, plan to attend some baseball games, or go bowling. If it's music or the arts, attend a concert, a live children's theater production, or be their audience and invite the neighbors for a concert *they* give for you.

In between, plan for some outings that will teach the grandchildren something while they are having fun. Take brief trips to a space, art, or science museum or to a factory where glass is blown, toys are carved, or candy is made. Get a library book about sea creatures to take along on a trip to the aquarium or one about exotic animals before a visit to the zoo.

If the brother and sister have different or conflicting ideas on what constitutes fun, try separating them. Each of you take one grandchild and go your separate ways, then share the excitement when you get home. You may be playing a board game with your granddaughter while your husband shoots hoops with his grandson.

If you post the month's schedule on your refrigerator, the children can see what is coming up. Don't overplan. For the month, schedule only two or three major events per week. Spending quiet time with them will be as important and fruitful as constantly going and doing. Take walks with your grandchildren, and listen to them talk as you relax together.

Count on it. The first words out of their little mouths will be, "What are we going to do?" You'll be ready. Take pictures and videos that will be treasured memories of this month together.

Have fun!

Fun for Rainy Days

Q. I love to have my grandchildren at my home, but I run out of ideas to keep them busy, especially on rainy days, because they tend to argue. *A.* I don't know how many grandchildren you have or their ages, but putting any two grandchildren together on a rainy day can spell double trouble. "I'm bored!" "Me too!" "There's nothing to do!" Here are some thoughts for you:

Some children are fascinated for long periods of time with a screwdriver, a pair of pliers, and something to take apart. Give them an old clock that doesn't work anymore. Let them take it apart and put it back together again. If the clock has a cord, be sure to remove it for safety. Provide a tray or a basket for the various pieces. Children as young as four will enjoy this.

You can trust even small children these days with your computer. Turn it on, get them started, and let them play a game or write a story that makes for great reading later. If you don't have a computer, have a box of office supplies handy: transparent tape, paper clips, paper, pens or pencils, erasers, stapler, labels, and other supplies. Get them started with some creative ideas, and let their imaginations do the rest.

Do you have a button collection? Let your grandchild play the button match game. They can spend hours searching for the right button and get so happy when they make matches. They think they are really helping you. (They are!)

Do you empty your coin purse into a jar at home? Give the money to a grandchild to sort out into piles of pennies, nickels, dimes, and quarters. The child will learn about different coins as he or she plays.

Provide them with old magazines and scissors (blunt scissors for the very young). Give them categories like fruit, vegetables, animals, and furniture, and ask them to cut out items in each category. With a little "Grandma's Paste" (flour and water) or a glue stick, they can cut and paste the pictures on blank sheets of paper and take them home to Mom and Dad. Turn a creative grandchild loose with pencil and paper to write a poem for you. Jigsaw puzzles for various age groups are great, too, as are making paper airplanes and origami.

Get a huge box from the appliance store, one in which a refrigerator or a washer or dryer came, cut a door and a window in it, and let the kids color it with crayons or paint. Then watch how many happy hours they spend in their make-believe home.

Ah, the peace and quiet!

Taking Grandchildren on Car Trips

Q. We are planning on having our grandsons, ages four and six, for much of the summer, and we'll be taking them with us on several short car trips and one long one. They get along pretty well, but do you have any suggestions for keeping them content and controlled?

A. A tape player with earphones is always a winner. Before you leave, make a trip to the library for free cassette tapes of children's music and stories.

You might also take a tape recorder and let the children be tour guides as they ride. The tape of the trip would be a wonderful present for their parents, and, considering their ages, would probably be a riot to listen to.

Allow them to take pictures with their own disposable cameras, which can be purchased at a discount store. Take blank postcards, and encourage the children to draw a picture of something they have seen on the trip. Mail the cards to their parents, or let the children take them home themselves to display in their rooms.

A metal nine-by-thirteen-inch baking pan turned over makes a great desk on a child's lap. Covered with colorful magnets, the lap desk helps a child turn miles into smiles.

Have you seen those clear plastic shoe pouches you can hang on the back of your closet door? (There's usually room for eight to twelve pairs of shoes.) Pick one up at any discount store and hang it on the back of the driver's seat, within easy reach of the children. In one pouch, put a healthful snack. Another might contain an inflatable ball or a jump rope for playing with at the next rest stop. Still another might hold a small pencil and pad. As a variation, you can divide the number of miles in the trip by the number of pouches. When you have traveled so many miles, the child can have whatever is in the next pouch. When the last item is retrieved, the trip is over, and everybody is happy!

Safety is of the utmost importance on car trips. Get written permission, signed by a parent, for any necessary medical care for the grandchildren. Also have an emergency telephone number with you at all times.

Be sure to ask the parent important questions about allergies. An unknown allergy could result in a medical emergency.

Supervise every minute! A young child can move out of sight in the blink of an eye. Walk around your car before getting in to make sure one of the children is not there.

And buckle up! It's a grandparenting law!

Fun without Getting Physically Exhausted

Q. My grandkids expect me to romp around with them. Physically, I just can't do some of what they expect, but I don't want to disappoint them. Do you have any ideas?

A. "I'm not as young as I used to be!" Most of us have said that once or twice. However, that doesn't have to stop you from having fun with the grandchildren:

- Try creative Bible reading: For example, say, "I'll be Mary. You be Martha," and let the child read her lines. Reading aloud helps the words and their meaning sink in.
- Make a deck of cards out of Scripture verses on three-by-five-inch cards. Ask your grandchild to shuffle them, then each of

you, in turn, pick a card from the deck. One side of each card shows the referenced verse, e.g., John 3:16. The other side shows the entire verse: "For God so loved the world . . ." One person draws a card and gives the verse reference. The other quotes the verse as your partner checks the verse from the other side of the card. This is good training and lots of fun.

- Pull out and dust off the family photo albums and other mementos you can explore with your grandchildren. You can while away hours and hours as you teach the child more about the family. Tell about your early life. Children especially like stories about when their parents were young and got into trouble or did something funny.
- Play board games that stretch their imaginations and teach them something about fair play, themselves, and their world.
- Go for walks if you can. A walk in the woods can be thrilling for a child. Play "pretend" as you walk. Now you are a rock. Then a tree. Enjoy the sky, clouds, and the breeze. Listen for birds and other creatures in the brush. Bring along a book to identify flowers, birds, or trees.
- Think ahead. Substitute your physical involvement with crafts, coloring, music, or other activities you can oversee. Build your grandchild's self-esteem by making him or her the leader, the initiator. Applaud their efforts with joy!

Letting Them Win

Q. Our granddaughters are five and seven and are very competitive with one another. Their poor parents have quite a time with them and, I think, give in to them far too much. I watch all this unfold during my visits.

I enjoy playing board games with the girls, but unlike their mother, I don't hold back on my turn and let them win. I just don't think it's right. What do you think?

A.   I agree with you. I've had some heated discussions with grandparents on this subject, but I'm sticking to my guns. Some grandparents think that allowing a child to win builds his self-esteem and serves to deepen the bonds of the relationship. There are other ways to accomplish those results.

It's a matter of honesty. Also, playing it straight when they lose teaches children to strive, to compete, and to win the next time. That spirit is reinforced when the grandparent cheers the child on for the next round.

Most important, not giving in to the temptation of letting a grandchild win teaches how to be a good loser as well as a good winner. As grandchildren grow up, their lives will be filled with such lessons.

The child who repeatedly gets angry and resentful when he loses should quit playing that particular game until he is older. Choose games to play with grandchildren that are fun for their age level and games that have been on the market for years, proving their appeal.

Congratulations! By teaching your grandchild in this small way that losing is part of life, you are helping to build a firm footing upon which your grandchild can stand against whatever comes.

SURROGATE GRANDPARENTING

A Win-Win Situation

Q.   I'm a widow, and I want to tell you about a sweet, little five-year-old and her three-year-old brother. Their only grandmother was killed in a home accident last year, and I took special care to love and nurture them when they came to my Sunday school room at church. The relationship grew, and I was invited to the children's home for dinner one Sunday. I would read to the children before dinner, play a game, and listen to them about their little problems and fears. I told them how I would handle things as a missionary in the days gone by.

One Sunday, the parents asked me if I would like to be a "surrogate grandparent" to the children. I didn't really know what that meant, but when they explained that it was nothing written down except on the heart, I accepted gladly. Now I go over every other Sunday and am invited for Christmas and other holiday celebrations. I love these children as if they were my own, and they love me. I know they do! I cannot put into words the joy they have brought into my life. Please tell others, and maybe another lonely person can have the blessing of a child in his or her life.

A. I'm glad to spread this good word. For families missing the love and sharing of a grandparent and for lonely senior adults, surrogate grandparenting is an idea for our time.

Thousands of parents say, "We would give almost anything we own for a genuine grandparent relationship for our child." Grandparents are missing for a variety of reasons:

- There are none on either side of the family.
- The real grandparents have died.
- The real grandparents don't keep in touch.

Young people need older people to talk to, play with, hug, listen to, giggle, and be silly with. They also need to learn from their elders' vast storehouse of wisdom and life experiences.

On the other hand, thousands of older people who have no natural grandchildren are missing out on the joys of grandparenting, longing for a loving relationship with no strings attached.

Potential grandparents are everywhere! The best place to look is within your own family—an older aunt, uncle, sister, or brother-in-law, a senior adult who would covenant with a parent in a grandparent-grandchild relationship. Is there a lonesome family member just waiting to share his or her life with a little one?

Another source might be the person next door or down the street who has demonstrated a loving attitude toward a child, the frequent senior-aged baby-sitter your child adores, or the widow or widower you know, for whom grandparenting a child would fill a great void.

Good friends can be surrogate grandparents. Retired teachers and missionaries like yourself make wonderful grandparents.

As in any new relationship of a personal nature, there are cautions:

- Adopt no strangers! Recruit only that person who has proved over time that he cares about the child and can be trusted. Know the person well.
- Make no promises. If there is verbal agreement, go slowly as you include the new addition to the family in happy times together.
- Likewise, the grandparent must keep his or her place in the agreement, abiding by the parent's instruction in every circumstance.

Think about an "Adopt-a-Grandchild" or surrogate grandparenting program for your church. If your pastor agrees, place a notice in the Sunday bulletin, and see if people respond.

Chosen carefully and supported by love and prayer, a surrogate grandparent can bring lasting blessings to a child and to themselves.

Sad Times

Illness

Loss

Abortion

Sad Times

Faith is the bird that sings
to greet the dawn while it is still dark.

FAY ANGUS[1]

How MUCH MORE WE LEAN ON THE EVERLASTING arms when we are in despair over a critically ill grandchild for whom the doctors have done all that can be done and to no avail! By losing a grandchild to God's divine plan, we lose also the potential that life held, the dreams and achievements of which we hoped to be an integral part.

At sad times like these, grandparents are called upon to summon an inner strength borne of maturity and experience, to stand with grieving children when we ourselves also mourn the loss.

In section 8, we see how we can triumph over such loss by practical action and by faith, even over the death of an adult child or our life partner.

When the unconscionable act of abortion invades our grandparenting season, Christian grandparents can find the strength to endure, trusting in the Lord's plan for their lives.

The sad times that try our souls may also try our faith in God. But the Comforter is ever present, our solace in the dark night.

ILLNESS

The Critically Ill Grandchild

Q. Our ten-year-old grandson has acute lymphocytic leukemia. He lives in another city and will undergo chemotherapy for two years. How can I support him through this time?

A. The word *leukemia* is frightening to all of us, but I want you to be encouraged. Leukemia survival figures have risen over the last thirty years from 4 percent to 73 percent. Cancer is the leading cause of death by disease in children, but it is getting rarer all the time with less than fifteen hundred children dying from cancer last year.[2] This is hopeful information for you to share with the parents and to hold on to yourself.

Call the Cancer Information Center of the National Cancer Institute to order its free pamphlets: *What You Need to Know about Leukemia, Someone in Your Family Has Cancer*, and *Young People with Cancer*. Reading these will help you understand the disease and treatment.

Your grandson will need more from you than phone calls. Although they should be made frequently, phone calls are mostly for the parents. Send him small presents, a deck of cards, origami paper and an instructional booklet, a hand puzzle, or an age-appropriate toy. Read a book into a cassette tape recorder, one chapter at a time, and mail the tape and the book. You might also record favorite Bible verses with your own commentary that uplifts and encourages.

Mail one card a week, a special one, perhaps homemade and silly. If you are an artist, the cards could depict something going on in your life. Cards like these help divert your grandson's attention from his condition, if only for a short time. Mailing them regularly will give him something to look forward to.

Pray faithfully for your grandson as you send your love and concern in various ways. Prayer is your best defense because, like all of us, your grandson is in God's hands.

Loss

The Death of a Grandchild

Q. We've lost a beloved grandchild. He was only six when he was hit by a car while riding his little bike. It's been two years now, and we still grieve. How have other grandparents coped with such terrible losses?

A. My heart hurts for you. We go through many trials in a lifetime. The valleys are as much a part of grandparenting as are the mountaintops, and giving up a grandchild to God's divine plan is one of the deepest valleys we could pass through. But you can pass through, and you will.

There is no timetable for grief. Reaching out for help is normal and healthy because you will feel this loss for many years to come, and to some degree, for a lifetime.

Consider Barbara and Marvin, whose lives were twice changed by drunk drivers. One nearly killed both of them. Then, nine years later, while still coping with their debilitating injuries, another drunk driver took the lives of their only son and their grandson. Barbara said, "One drunk driver broke my bones; the other one broke my heart. My only peace comes from knowing that I don't know all of the answers, but someday I will."

Evelyn lost her sixteen-year-old granddaughter to gun violence. In an instant, a teenager with a stolen gun snuffed out the brilliant future of one of Evelyn's reasons for living. She had promised Amy a car if she did not smoke or drink. Instead, she bought her a funeral. Evelyn said, "God has promised me that I will see Amy again."

Grandma and Grandpa Hasselblad lost two grandsons to SIDS (Sudden Infant Death Syndrome). They said, "Both Jordan and Jacob enriched our lives, and in the brief time we had them, we recognized their special qualities. We don't ask why. "Why" questions are for SIDS, not for God. We are slowly learning to accept what has happened and can feel God's love from the people around us."

Another grandparent offered, "My grandchild had a chance to be loved by parents who wanted him and who prayed for his coming. He brought great happiness to the hearts of both sets of grandparents and to all who knew him."

When a grandchild dies

- Allow people to talk about the child.
- Accept the funeral service as a time for the whole family to grieve together and say good-bye.
- Accept people's expressions of love, even when their words don't come out right. The intent is there.
- Support the parents and siblings.
- Remember that God's love is present in crises.
- It is OK to grieve.[3]

Standing by Grieving Children

Q. There are no words to describe my pain when our grandbaby was born, only to die shortly after, right there in the hospital. They cleaned her up, and put her in a little pink blanket. She was so beautiful. I just got to hold her and then give her back. It hurt so much, but I know it hurts my daughter and son-in-law even more.

Do you have any suggestions of how I can be of support to them? I pray for them every day.

A. Your prayers for your children will be a powerful source of comfort when nothing else can penetrate their pain. Your patience with their moods as they grieve will bring you closer in your shared sorrow. And practical helps will cheer them through the difficult times of remembering.

One mother wrote, "Mother was here. She stayed with me but she knew when to leave me alone. When friends who had also lost children came to visit me, she left us alone."

Another gave this poignant recollection: "My dad was there at the right time. He didn't say anything. He just looked at my husband, put his big arms around him, and held him. My husband broke into tears. I had never seen him cry like that. It was a real hard cry. It was like he needed the support of a man to understand and hold him without saying anything."

One couple, who had two losses, was touched by the grandfather's desire to help bury their second son. "Dad said, 'I am going to do it. I want to do it for my grandson.' It felt so good for him to say 'my grandson.'"

June Cerza Kolf, in her book *Grandma's Tears, Comfort For Grieving Grandparents*, reminds us to allow ourselves as grandparents to go through the grieving process as we support the parents:

> Because you are one of the older generation, you may feel you should have all the right answers or a secret formula to ease everyone else's pain. However, it is not possible for one individual to have all the answers. Forgive yourself for not knowing what to say or for not having perfect words of comfort to offer. You are hurting, too, and to lay guilt on yourself at this time is fruitless.[4]

The Death of an Adult Child

Q. Our family is mourning the recent death of my daughter at age thirty-six from diabetes. Even though the process of losing her was a long one, and there was time to say good-bye, it is still very, very hard for my grandsons, ages eleven and thirteen. They come and they cry and ask questions. How should I try to explain it to them?

A. Children, even young ones, can understand death when the subject is treated honestly and sympathetically. Answer their questions that way. Your grandchildren will mourn visibly for at least a year, then within, out of sight, for many years to come. They will need more grandparent hugs now and your encouragement to talk about their mother and remember the good times. Be upbeat about their futures, and assure their sense of well-being by demonstrating your love and thoughtfulness.

Above all, listen to them, not just to what they say but to their body language and how they say the words. Their fears and pain must not be rationalized or covered up but addressed either by you, another family member, or a professional counselor. Listening is your gift to them at this terrible time in their young lives.

You have experienced this loss too. The death of a loved one, whether sudden or over a long illness, is a shattering experience, and your life will not be the same.

Take good care of yourself. Get enough rest, eat properly, and exercise. Allow yourself to go through the stages of grief as you help your grandsons do the same.

The Death of a Spouse

Q. My husband and I were married for fifty-one years. He passed away one year ago this Friday. We have a loving family of four children, nine grandchildren, and two great-grandchildren, all of whom have been very supportive to me. Everybody seems to have gone their own way now after it's been a year, but to me, it doesn't go away.

I still can't bring myself to take his clothes to the church collection box. I suffer silently because I don't want to bother the children. I feel so alone. My sister says I have to snap out of it, but she's still got her husband.

A. The loss of your life's mate has made you numb. This is perfectly normal, and there is no time limit on the numbness. There are ways, however, to begin to heal and regain a good feeling about living, even to forget for a period of time. We do not forget our loved ones, but the pain of the loss can be lessened.

The best way to make that happen is to reach out to others. Choosing to put grief to work actually helps us heal as we help someone else. Become active on a church committee, help in the children's Sunday school or day-care area. Working with young people has a way of cheering the spirit and restoring hope for the future. Get back to the business of living your life. Give in to your sister. Let her help you. Tell her you'll try.

Keep memories of your husband alive by displaying pictures in your home. I know women who talk to their husband's picture every day. Talking *about* him to others is therapeutic and will become less painful as time goes by.

It is time to give away his personal effects. Ask a son or daughter to go through them with you. Allow yourself to cry. Try to think of happy times as you do this.

Depend on God and His promises. Isaiah 40:31 is a special source of strength:

> But those who hope in the Lord
> will renew their strength.
> They will soar on wings like eagles;
> they will run and not grow weary,
> they will walk and not be faint.

AT THE PLACE OF THE SEA

> Have you come to the Red Sea place in your life,
> Where, in spite of all you can do,
> There is no way out, there is no way back,
> There is no other way, but through?
>
> Then wait on the Lord, with a trust serene,
> Till the night of your fear is gone;

He will send the winds, He will heap the floods,
When He says to your soul,
"Go on!"

And His hand shall lead you through, clear through,
Ere the watery walls roll down;
No wave can touch you, no foe can smite,
No mightiest sea can drown.
The tossing billows may rear their crests,
Their foam at your feet may break,
But over their bed you shall walk dry-shod
In the path that your Lord shall make.

In the morning watch, 'neath the lifted cloud,
You shall see but the Lord alone,
When He leads you forth from the place of the sea,
To a land that you have not known.
And your fears shall pass as your foes have passed,
You shall no more be afraid;
You shall sing His praise in a better place.
In a place that His hand hath made.

—Annie Johnson Flint[5]

ABORTION

A Grandparenting Tragedy

Q. We have learned that our only daughter had an abortion following her divorce and that there were complications, which means she probably cannot ever have another child. This means I will never be a grandparent, and I am devastated. Don't girls realize that when they do this desperate thing, they affect so many more lives down the line than their own?

A.   It is safer today to live on death row than to live in a mother's womb. Abortion is the scourge of modern society. In the United States, more than a million and a half abortions are performed each year, a figure that doesn't reflect all of them since some states don't keep track. Every abortion takes at least one life and affects the lives of countless other family members and friends forever, first of all, the mother.

No, some women don't realize all of these consequences when they are making this despicable choice out of fear, anger, selfishness, or rebellion.

If you haven't already done so, go to your daughter and offer your loving support. Avoid harsh criticism of the act, but do not attempt to hide the depth of your loss. Pray about this meeting, and only go to her when you have peace about it. An angry confrontation will do no good, only harm.

Never say never! God may have other plans for your daughter. Until the day He decides you will be given a biological grandchild, occupy yourself by loving other people's children. Surrogate grandparent programs are being offered in churches all over the country, programs that bring together children who have no grandparents and senior adults who need a child in their lives.

There is always hope according to God's Word:

> For I know the plans I have for you,
> says the LORD,
> plans for welfare and not for evil,
> to give you a future and a hope.
> Jeremiah 29:11, RSV

Keep that hope alive as you show your love and compassion to others.

Bad Times

Bad Times

Sin is not hurtful because it is forbidden.
It is forbidden because it is hurtful.

BENJAMIN FRANKLIN[1]

T HE SINS OF OUR CHILDREN CAUSE ANGUISH for grandparents who hurt for the child and for themselves. The questions in section 9 make it clear that use of illegal drugs, alcohol, and tobacco is ravaging relationships, and the rubble of the destruction falls on the small shoulders of innocent children.

Stopping the generational sins of alcohol and child abuse is also addressed in this section. It is heartening to see more leaders addressing these problems and working to reverse the trends. The church, so long in silence on these taboo subjects, has now joined the fight with helpful resources, referral programs, and counseling.

The impact of violence in our society on its children is also reversible if each one of us has the courage to speak the truth with conviction and translate our words to action. The growing consensus seems to be that we can move beyond talk and finally act to make America, once again, a safe place in which to raise a child. It will take more than a consensus, however. It will require an individual effort on the part of every single American to make it happen. I urge you to pick up your shield and go to war for the hearts and souls of our children.

DRUG ADDICTION

When Parents Abuse Drugs

Q. My husband and I raised our kids in a Christian home. Both of them did fine until they were introduced to crack cocaine by another family member.

One married a girl after she became pregnant, but she took off, leaving our son with a three-year-old boy. The other, our daughter, married an older man who left her pregnant after two years. I was the childbirth coach when my granddaughter was born.

Today we have two grandchildren, each of them living in needy single-parent homes. We spend our days and nights in fear that the children will be harmed, left alone, or worse. Our son and daughter refuse to listen to our pleas for counseling or drug rehabilitation. They're both very good at putting on a show for other people that everything's all right, but we know differently, and we see and hear a lot when we have their children, which is often. They say they are good parents and love their children, but they're both in denial as to the extent of their drug use and tend to gang up on us in defense of their lifestyles. When we try to talk to them, we are angrily accused of meddling and told to mind our own business.

We feel helpless and heartsick. We have tremendous guilt feelings that something in our parenting caused it all. How can we change this dangerous situation without being preachy and cutting ourselves off from a relationship with our grandchildren?

A. Let's deal with the guilt feelings first. You did not give birth to two drug addicts. Each one of your children chose this lifestyle. The extent to which they abuse substances is something over which you have no control, and you probably did nothing to cause it. Parents who have never taken a drink of alcohol or an illegal pill in their lives may have a drug-addicted child. Conversely, some who do abuse drugs raise sober, upstanding children. You didn't do this; they are doing it to themselves.

You mentioned that you raised your children in a Christian home. Christian principles are in them. They know what they're doing, and no amount of preaching from anyone will help. You must realize there is little, if anything, you can do to change the situation. I know that is not what you want to hear, but it is a fact. You can't change their behavior, and you can't force them to seek help. *They must do it.*

You might research a list of rehabilitation centers and counselors in your area and give it to your children, but they will have to make the decision to go. Some counselors advise parents to give up hope. However, Christians know there is always hope through prayer. Give your son and daughter's addiction and behavior problems to God in prayer. Release yourself of them because you can't change them. You may only drive your children and grandchildren further away if you try.

Now, to the grandchildren. Once you've shed the guilt that you might be responsible for what is happening, put on a new attitude toward your children to ensure that you will have a continuing influence in your grandchildren's lives. You can be a life link for them as time goes by. Be with them as often as possible. Do not coax information from them but listen as they grow older. Be a port in the storm when something goes wrong. Supply basic needs such as extra food, warm clothing in winter, etc. Toss in some entertainment when you can, and have fun with your grandchildren. This new attitude will be noticed by your children, and who knows? Turning a new leaf in how you deal with this whole situation for the sake of your grandchildren may be the catalyst to turning your children toward help and a better future for all of you.

Addicted Grandchildren

Q. Christmas Eve this year was the unhappiest night of our lives. For years, our home has been the holiday gathering place for our daughter and son-in-law and their two children, now ages fifteen and eighteen. This year, both teenagers were absent.

The girl has run off to be with her druggie friends. She "huffs" gasoline and glue to get high and smokes marijuana. Our grandson, who has been rebelling for years, told his parents he doesn't believe in Christmas anymore. He still lives at home. His parents suspect that he has experimented with LSD, and they suspect that he is selling drugs because he always has money.

Our heart breaks for our daughter and son-in-law, who have been good, loving parents and are at the end of their rope. What can we do to support them and help our grandchildren before it's too late?

A. This is a family crisis that requires the support of all family members. The parents may need your help to locate and bring back the girl. Then, suggest that the parents consider calling a family meeting, inviting extended family who live close enough to come. Tell them they can use the regular gathering place—your home.

Come up with a plan, perhaps with each willing family member playing a particular role. For example, an aunt and uncle might invite both young people for dinner and a serious talk; a sister- in-law might get closer to the teenage girl, becoming a mentor and confidant. This is a scriptural approach to resolution. There's a very real chance that all of this effort will be to no avail, but you will have tried every avenue.

An extreme but often effective alternative is *intervention.* An intervention is a planned surprise confrontation of the person and can be accomplished only by hiring a professional facilitator who is experienced in drug addiction therapy. You can learn more about intervention by inquiring at a reputable counseling office or psychological clinic in your area.

Keep in close contact with the parents, offering prayer support; they will need it to get through this tragedy. I realize it is little consolation to know that you are one of hundreds of thousands of grandparents who live through the nightmare of their grandchildren's drug addictions. You can help by not overreacting, being a positive role model, and building your grandchildren's self-esteems.

Show the depth of your love by standing together as a family.

Keeping Grandchildren Drug-Free

Q. There is so much drug use among our young people. How can I help to keep my grandchildren free of drugs? They are twelve and fourteen years old.

A. In the 1980s, there was a steady decline in the use of alcohol and other drugs among young people, ages twelve to seventeen. After a decade of significant progress, however, a recent survey indicates that this downward trend has leveled off for some drugs, leaving the rate of alcohol and other drug use in the United States still high.[2]

The reasons for drug use are varied. Children may use drugs to satisfy their curiosity, conform to peer pressure, relieve anxiety, or have an adventure. But, whatever tempts them, we must teach our children to reject drugs because drug use is illegal and harmful, and interferes with academic, social, and spiritual development.

Drug information programs, while important, cannot stand alone as a deterrent to drug use. It is the responsibility of the parents to educate and inform their children of the devastating consequences of drug experimentation and continued use. A grandparent's role is to support the parents by being aware of current trends and by building a high self-esteem in their grandchildren. It has been proven that a teen who has good self-esteem is better able to resist the temptation of drugs.

- Teach your grandchildren to say no to drugs by talking openly with them. Educate yourself on the subject so that you have accurate information to share.
- Take a look at your own use of tobacco and alcohol for the messages you may be sending.
- Find ways to honor your grandchildren often for all the good things they do.
- Monitor friends when grandchildren are with you. Peer pressure is one of the top reasons a child slips and falls into the drug culture.

For more information on drug prevention, contact the American Council for Drug Education, 204 Monroe Street, Suite 110, Rockville, MD 20850.

DANGEROUS HABITS

Smoking

Q. I have been married to a great guy for thirty-two years. He's fun, smart, caring, and a deacon in our church. The problem is that he smokes —a lot. We've all tried to get him to quit, but he says he enjoys it. I'm very concerned for his health, and with all we now know about the dangers of secondhand smoke, I am concerned for myself, the whole family, but most of all our two-year old grandson, who thinks the sun rises and sets over my husband's head. The two of them are inseparable. He says he won't smoke around our grandson, but I know he does. I've seen him in the garage. What can I do?

A.   Tell him that secondhand smoke is responsible for 150,000 to 300,000 serious respiratory ailments each year in children under eighteen months of age and for up to 26,000 new cases of childhood asthma each year. Studies show that parental or peer smoking contributes to the initiation of a smoking habit in a young person. Tell him that nonsmoking women who are exposed to a moderate amount of secondhand smoke at home face a 30 percent increased risk of lung cancer; those living with a heavy smoker, an 80 percent increased risk; and those exposed at work, a 39 percent increased risk.[3]

These are the facts. A television commercial over twenty years ago showed a young dad being followed on the beach by his small son who stretched his little legs far to place his feet into the footsteps his daddy was making in the sand. When they arrived at the beach umbrella, the dad stretched out, put his hands behind his head, closed his eyes, and yawned. His son lay down, placed his pudgy hands behind his head, and yawned, all the while keeping an eye on his beloved father. The dad stirred, reached for his shirt, and took a pack of cigarettes out, selected one, placed it in his mouth, lit it, and took a deep breath in and out. His son lay on his back, holding an imaginary pack of cigarettes and an imaginary match, lit an unseen cigarette, and breathed in and out—just like his daddy.

Just as parents do, grandparents have an awesome responsibility to be healthy models for our grandchildren, protecting them and not exposing them to harm. For his health and that of his family, continue to try to convince your husband to quit. Your best ammunition is the truth. The life-threatening dangers of smoking and secondhand smoke are now widely known.

> Children imitate the ones they love,
> and they love their grandparents.

Drinking

Q. Please help me. We are the grandparents of a ten-year-old boy and a twelve-year-old girl who love their grandfather very much. However, as my husband has grown older, he has not taken his losses very well, finding his solutions and consolation in heavy drinking. He becomes loud and uses foul language around the children. I know it would break his heart if the grandchildren didn't come to see him, but I know his drinking habit is the reason they and their parents don't come as often as they used to.

I'm tired of making excuses for him. What should I do?

A. Excuses mask the problem, and your husband clearly has one. Honesty is the best policy. You don't need to make a big scene. Pick your time to talk to him—never at night after he has been drinking during the day. Tell him how his drinking changes him, and that, as much as they love him, the grandchildren are uncomfortable when he is loud and uses foul language.

He won't like it, but he'll hear you. If he doesn't get too defensive, ask him gently to do two things for you: First, ask him to go to an open meeting of your city's Alcoholics Anonymous to see if he is an alcoholic. (Offer to go with him.) Second, ask him to get a physical exam for two reasons: to check his physical condition and to check for depression. The losses that come with age can bring on serious depression, and that combined with the abuse of alcohol can be deadly.

If his addiction continues unabated, he risks malnutrition as the alcohol replaces more nutritious sources of energy and inhibits the function of some digestive organs. He also risks liver cirrhosis, hepatitis, heart disease, gastritis, and cancers of the respiratory tract.

Understand that this is your husband's problem, not yours. Reassure him that you and the children love him very much and will pray for him and help in any way you can.

Telling him the truth will be difficult for you, but it is your best first step to truly helping him and to ensuring a future relationship with your children and grandchildren.

Generational Alcohol Abuse

Q. My father-in-law was an alcoholic who died of liver disease. My husband was an alcoholic who was abusive to me and the children. We are divorced. Now, my son, age twenty-two, is an alcoholic, an angry young man who refuses therapy. He and his wife have a volatile marriage that could blow up any day, effecting my one-year-old granddaughter.

How can we stop this generational sin?

A. You might be the first person in your family to ask that important question. Good for you!

The Bible says in Exodus that the sins of the fathers are passed on to the children through the third and fourth generations. This happens, not because God doesn't love grandchildren but because it is a basic principle of human nature.

The hallmark of addiction is denial. Your son knows about his grandfather and his father; he's in denial about himself. He needs to be forced to recognize that he needs help and to seek counseling. Who in the family could best get through to him? Probably his wife.

You and your daughter-in-law should attend an open meeting of your local chapter of Alcoholics Anonymous. There you will learn new skills and ways to convince your son to seek help. Your daughter-in-law may be encouraged to present options to her husband, even including a separation that keeps him from his child if he doesn't get help. Drastic decisions are sometimes necessary to stop the generational abuse that will otherwise continue unchecked.

It would be a good idea for you and your daughter-in-law to see a qualified Christian counselor as well, someone who can help you understand what has happened so it will not happen again. The last thing you want is to watch your granddaughter grow up and repeat her father's pattern.

ENDING THE MADNESS

Stopping Child Abuse

Q. My daughter is twenty, got divorced about a year ago, and has custody of our two grandchildren, even though she has a court-documented history of abusing one of them. The children's father is in prison. Another man is living with her. I rarely get the kids, ages three and eighteen months, and when I do, I see bruises on them. Their mother says the bruises were caused by a fall.

I don't know what is the matter with her, but it nearly kills me to see the scared looks in the three-year-old's eyes, and the little one is stone quiet and withdrawn.

I didn't raise my daughter to be like this. She just went the way of the world when she became a teenager and got in with the wrong crowd.

I don't see anything I can do for her, but isn't there something I can do for the grandchildren to keep them safe?

I had Child Protective Services investigate the home once. They called back saying everything was fine. Can you believe it? If I do that again, I know she will never let me see the children again. How do they define *child abuse*, so I can convince CPS this is what's happening?

A.   *Child abuse* is defined as harm to or neglect of a child under the age of eighteen, caused by acts or omissions of the parents or persons responsible for the child's welfare or any person residing in the same household, or by the parent's boyfriend or girlfriend. It may include

- serious physical injury unexplained by available medical history as accidental; or
- serious mental injury unexplained by available medical history as accidental; or
- sexual abuse or sexual exploitation; or
- serious physical neglect.

Child abuse does *not* usually include harm done to the child solely as a result from environmental factors such as inadequate housing, income, furnishings, clothing, or medical care that is beyond the control of the birth parents or other persons responsible for the child's welfare.[4]

Start documenting everything you see and hear. Take pictures, although showing authorities a picture of bruises isn't enough without proof that the injuries could be only the result of abuse, which must be documented by a third party.

With a friend, drop in to see the children unannounced. Later, write down what you saw and heard and have the friend sign it as a witness. You can do the same thing when you have the children at your house.

When you've gathered several such documents, carefully dated and timed, take them to a family law attorney who is experienced in child abuse cases. Follow his or her instructions.

Remember that alerting the state child protective authorities to your suspicions of child abuse can result in the child going into foster care and not home with you, as some grandparents erroneously think will automatically be the case. Begin with a private family law attorney. It will be worth the money to get legal advice on how to proceed.

With some wayward adult sons and daughters, the only way to effect a change in their behavior is to shock them with the truth. Gather the truth, and take it to an attorney. Hopefully, your work will stop any harm from happening to your grandchildren and will result in your daughter getting professional counseling.

Violence in Society

Q. We live a normal, peaceful life in retirement after raising three fine children who have married and given us five wonderful grandchildren. We did not particularly shelter our children from the world. We just raised them with Christian principles and did our best to prepare them. I know they are doing the same for their children, but we can't help but worry about our grandchildren growing up in a society where violence seems to be so prevalent. How can we help protect them?

A. The facts about escalating violence in America are alarming and might overwhelm any grandparents with paralyzing fear for their grandchildren's future . . .

Except for the Christian grandparents. We don't have to be *victims* of violence. We can be *victors* over violence because we have Christ who gave us the victory, even over death! The writer of Hebrews reminds us:

> Let us fix our eyes on Jesus, the author and perfecter of our faith, who for the joy set before him endured the cross, scorning its shame, and sat down at the right hand of the throne of God. Consider him who endured such opposition from sinful men, so that you will not grow weary and lose heart.
>
> Hebrews 12:2-3

To fix our eyes on the negative fuels our fears for the safety and well-being of our grandchildren. We see possible harm around every corner, and we don't trust God to keep them safe.

Protection of the children is the job of the parent. Grandparents can support the parent's efforts, be available for counsel and advice, and keep current on trends and remedies. The most important way a grandparent can help a grandchild in this violent society is to be a willing listener. We can consistently reinforce safety measures taught by their parents, point to Jesus Christ as Protector, and demonstrate our trust in Him by word and example.

Be a source of joy and positive thinking for your grandchildren, who need the strength of your humor and love more than any previous generation. Be alert for any contribution you can make in your community to help bring an end to societal violence in the twenty-first century.

FACTS

- Unintentional injury and heart disease declined from 1980 to 1991 by 25.2 percent and 18.1 percent, respectively. During the same period, firearm-related injuries and deaths increased by 13.6 percent.
- Gun-related death is expected to rise to become the highest cause of death in America from 1992–2002.
- Suicide and homicide combined as the third leading cause of death in 1991.[5]
- Every fifteen seconds a woman is beaten. As many as four million suffer from and nearly four thousand women die of abuse each year.[6]

Violence in the Media

Q. What is your opinion of the role media play in the escalation of violence in our country today?

A.   Philippians 4:8 instructs us: "Whatever is true, whatever is noble, whatever is right, whatever is pure, whatever is lovely, whatever is admirable—if anything is excellent or praiseworthy—think about such things."

Do you really think your grandchildren are going to remember that verse every time a television set is turned on? Every time they peruse the magazines in the barber's waiting room? Every time they walk into a movie with friends? It's Pollyannaish to think that they will. Worse yet, some of our grandchildren have been so duped by the entertainment industry that they *will not* make such a commitment.

Christian kids can become desensitized by exposure to profane, violent, and immoral media. All of the parental and grandparental love in the world cannot protect today's children from this onslaught, because it is everywhere they go—on television, in movies, magazines, and now, on computer.

I agree with nationally known warrior against media sex and violence, Michael Medved, who says, "Tens of millions of Americans now see the entertainment industry as an all-powerful enemy, an alien force that assaults our most cherished values and corrupts our children. The dream factory has become the poison factory."[7]

What can a grandparent do to defeat this powerful enemy?

- Limit and monitor a grandchild's television viewing.
- Provide healthy reading material in your home and as gifts to the child.
- Screen every movie before you see it with a grandchild.
- Write sponsors of offensive programming and publishers of offensive books and magazines. Let them know you will not continue to watch or read unless they discontinue their support of those media sources.
- Call or write your congressional and senatorial leaders, encouraging them to sponsor legislation requiring the Federal Communications Commission to more closely monitor sex and violence in media.

FACTS

- By the time the average child reaches high school graduation, he has spent more than eighteen thousand hours in front of the TV, far more than the twelve thousand or so hours he has spent in the classroom.
- Ninety-eight percent of all American households own television sets, the highest rate of ownership in the world. Sixty percent of those households subscribe to cable. Americans own seventy-two million videocassette recorders.
- Televised violence has a clear and reproducible effect on the behavior of children and contributes to the frequency with which violence is used to resolve conflict and the passivity with which violence is perceived.[8]

Grandparenting Challenges

CUSTODY AND VISITATION

OTHER CHALLENGES

Grandparenting Challenges

"My grandfather always said that
living is like licking honey off a thorn."

Louis Adamic[1]

Writer Susan Lenzkes puts life's challenges in perspective:

> Life is sharp. It pierces with good-byes, . . . tear-stained cheeks, . . . rejection, wrinkles, . . . broken promises, broken dreams, broken hearts, broken lives. God's children are not at home here; but we are here nonetheless. And we discover that it's impossible to enjoy this world's sunshine without enduring its clouds and storms.[2]

One such storm is the aftermath of your child's divorce. The parent of your grandchild who is going through the rigors of divorce probably isn't thinking about the fact that you and the other set of grandparents may also be divorcing as well. Losing long and dear in-law friendships through the divorce of our children is but one of the grandparent challenges highlighted by questions in section 10.

Becoming dependent in old age is a challenge that may require a grandparent to live under the same roof with a child or grandchild's family. Step-grandparenting joys and fears combine to make life more interesting for seniors with enough love to go around. Another unique opportunity exists in a foster care situation, in which a grandparent has a chance to temporarily model an everlasting faith for a child who has been beaten up by the system and comes with little or nothing he can trust.

It is hard to imagine a more difficult challenge than to have to go to court against your own child in a fight for custody of your grandchild or when visitation of a beloved grandchild has been taken away unjustly. This section also answers questions about adoption of a grandchild and what can be done when efforts to protect the best interest of your grandchild are to no avail.

Once again we take a motivation check to ensure that our true aim is what is right for the child and not just for ourselves.

CUSTODY AND VISITATION

Filing for Custody

Q. My husband and I are in our mid-sixties and are considering filing for legal custody of our five-year-old granddaughter. She lives in an unstable, possibly dangerous single-parent home, but she has been living with us on a temporary guardianship for the past year. Can you tell us what is involved in applying for legal custody and some of the problems we may face?

A. Filing for custody begins with *pleadings* or documents filed by yourself or your attorney in court. At the end of your pleadings, you should close with a paragraph telling the judge what it is you want him or her to do. Sign all documents and type in your name, address, and phone number. If you are handling the procedure yourself, check with the court clerk for the appropriate forms, and a docket or case number will be assigned to your case.

In some states, you may need to file a financial statement with the court. The two main purposes for this would be to show that you have the financial ability to care for your grandchild and for the court to determine the amount of child support the parents should pay to you. The next step is notification of this action to other parties involved (usually the parents). Then begin preparing your evidence.

If you choose to seek custody without benefit of an attorney, rest assured it can be done. A helpful book that you can order from your local bookstore is *Grandparent's Rights* by Traci Truly.

All states have requirements that grandparents must meet in order to obtain legal custody. You will have to establish that you have had significant past contacts with your grandchild. Assuming that the parents appear in court and contest your attempt, the greatest hurdle you will have to overcome is the *parental preference*. In an overwhelming majority of states, the court starts out presuming that the parents should have custody. The burden is on the grandparents to overcome that presumption. The "best interest of the child" is the determining factor.[3]

Grandparents seek legal custody because of abusive, neglectful, unstable, or absent parents. The judge will wonder whether the older grandparent will be physically able to care for the child until the child reaches adulthood. Your track record as a parent will be considered as will your relationship with your own children and your financial situation. You don't have to be wealthy, but the court wants to know whether or not you can meet the day-to-day requirements of raising a child for the years to come.

The Best Interest of the Child

Q. Our daughter-in-law has just about devastated us emotionally and financially. After our son was killed in a car accident, she became addicted to drugs and neglected our grandson, age seven-and-a-half, for years until we petitioned the court and got temporary custody of him two years ago. She was ordered to go into drug therapy. Well, we've been going to court against her for the past year. She says she is drug-free now, has a job, and wants our grandson back. We don't believe her and fear for the child if he goes back with her. She has the same friends, lives in the same awful place, and we don't think she's changed a bit.

We love our grandson so much, he's like our own. He's in Sunday school and preschool, takes swimming lessons, and plays with other kids in the neighborhood. We take him camping. We buy all of his clothes and medicines. Why should we give him back?

There's going to be a court hearing soon. What do you advise us to do to ensure that he will be safe with us?

A.   It doesn't matter what you believe about your daughter-in-law's rehabilitation from drugs or whether or not she is fit to raise her son. This is a matter for the court to decide, and, if she can prove she has complied with the court order, she will be awarded custody.

This will be a heartbreaking decision for you if it comes. You've done a wonderful job of caring for your grandson, but grandparents who become the primary caregivers to a grandchild know in their heart that the day may come when they will have to give him back. If that day comes for you, accept it, and do all you can to assist your grandson in the transition. If the court determines that your daughter-in-law deserves the right to parent her child, your grandson will need you as much as he ever has to be loving and supportive of him.

If the child goes back to his mother, monitor the new arrangement as closely as possible. Your attorney can advise you about actions you might take if and when problems arise.

The social service system and courts consider that the best interest of a child is served when the child resides with one or both parents. Caring, loving grandparents must put aside their own ideas of what they feel is right and good for the child and abide by the court's decision. Be as supportive as you can to your grandchild's mother. Then you will become a partner in the raising of your grandson and be able to continue some of the beautiful times you've had with him.

If, indeed, the mother has gotten her life straightened out, your grandson will grow up with a loving mother and a loving grandmother.

Don't be guilty of placing him between the two of you in an emotional tug-of-war. Swallow hard, and do what is best for him and not yourself.

Visitation and the Ex-Daughter-in-Law

Q. We lived near our only son and his wife during their nine-year marriage and had a wonderful relationship with our granddaughter, who is now seven. Last year our daughter-in-law had an affair, divorced our son, and won custody of our granddaughter. They are living with the man she was seeing, and my husband and I have received a letter saying she never again wants us to have anything to do with our granddaughter. We are heartsick over this. Is there anything we can do? Do we have any rights?

A. It will be of little comfort to know that you are one of many thousands of grandparents who have been robbed of a grandchild in a society devastated by broken promises and broken homes. It is a shame when family bickering and vindictiveness rob a child of the love of a grandparent. Studies have shown that multigenerational contact between children and grandparents, even great-grandparents, provides a special unconditional love and nurturing that is healthy for children.

All fifty states have laws that address the issues of grandparent visitation. In a divorce situation, under most state laws, a grandparent can file a request for visitation in the county and before the judge who granted the divorce. This is done by a "petition to intervene" and a "request for grandparent visitation" in accordance with that state's specific statute, and they will vary from state to state. Some states are more restrictive about grandparent visitation while others are quite liberal. Some permit visitation if you simply show the court that you have had a substantial past relationship with the child or that the visitation is in the child's best interest.[4]

Go to your local library, and read about your state's current law on visitation by grandparents, or contact your local state bar association for a referral to a family law attorney who is experienced in visitation matters. Interview him or her before you decide to proceed.

In seeking visitation of a grandchild, check your motivation for doing so to make sure it is in the best interest of the child, because that's the way the court will look at it. Gather all of the facts, and do your homework. Be confident of your rights in your state. It will be expensive emotionally and can be expensive financially as well.

When All Else Fails

Q. My son was killed in a car accident, and I have fought my son's widow for two years in court just for the privilege of visiting my grandson, who is now six. She and my son were not getting along when the accident happened, and she has made it plain that she intends to ignore our side of the family now.

I have no more money or energy for the fight. My grandson, whom I love so much, probably doesn't remember me by now. I pray for him every day. Do you have any suggestions?

A. It sounds like you've done all you can legally. It's time to start writing a journal, a personal journal for your grandson. Write to your grandchild about how you felt when he was born, how happy you were to have him come into your life, and how much you love him. Write only positive comments about his mother, even though you might be itching to tell him a few things. Write about how pretty she looked when he was born and what a good time you had together when he was brought home from the hospital.

Write down your traditional values, how and where you grew up, met, and married his grandfather. Write down memories of his dad, how much you loved him, and some of the things he did when he was a child, especially funny things.

A personal journal to your estranged grandchild is a last resort, but it may turn out to be the only way you can keep that all-important link. If you don't do something, the child will grow to adulthood with questions about his heritage that will never be answered. Among the most important will be questions about the kinds of illnesses in the family that took lives, illnesses he might be able to prevent if he has the knowledge.

This will be a difficult, emotional task. Take your time. When you feel that it is finished, place it in your safe deposit box, marked "To be opened by (your grandchild's full name) on the event of my death." Your executor will see that this document goes directly to your grandson.

It's a loving thing to do and good therapy for you. Your grandson will read it someday and know that you cared; despite anything he may have been told, he will know you loved him.

OTHER CHALLENGES

Lost Friendships

Q. When my daughter divorced and joined the ranks of single mothers, my husband and I lost more than a son-in-law. We lost a treasured, close, ten-year friendship with his parents.

The four of us used to go hunting and fishing together. We used to trade off on using our RVs and had some of the best times of our lives with them. We like the same things and got along just great.

The divorce was messy, fault on both sides. To my knowledge, none of us grandparents took sides. It just started to feel uncomfortable getting together because feelings were so tender one way or the other. The last time we were on a short trip, our son-in-law's mother didn't like what we were saying, which was only the truth about the situation, and left to go back to town by herself. That was the last time we've been together.

It's been almost a year. We miss them, and I'll bet they miss us, too, although they haven't contacted us. Do you think we should try to get back in touch with them?

A Yes, I do! Talk to your daughter about it. I'm surprised she hasn't mentioned it, knowing how close you four were. Then again, she may feel like closing the door on the past. That doesn't mean you have to.

Over this past year, perhaps one or both of them has come close to picking up the phone to call you but thought you wouldn't like it.

Tell your daughter you miss these folks, and see if she won't understand and give her blessing to reconnecting. If the other set of grandparents see your grandson from time to time, your daughter might be able to say something to them to smooth the way.

Be prepared to apologize first thing when you get them on the phone or see these friends in person. Obviously, something you or your husband said last time upset the other grandmother. Even if you don't know what that was, apologize for it. Make a pact between you that the subject of the divorce will never again be discussed.

The circumstances of some messy divorces can cause terrible rifts between the two sets of grandparents, deep chasms that probably cannot be bridged. It doesn't sound like the break in your relationship with this couple was that serious.

Dear friends are a treasure, and life is short. Go for it!

Dependency: Living with Family

Q. I am eighty-seven years old and a widow. I have lived with my granddaughter and her family for four years now.

Ever since I came here, I have felt as if I've been put on a shelf. I'm not important; I'm just ignored. My granddaughter works. I don't see her except at the dinner table and at church on Sundays when I am able to go. The three kids pretty much have the run of the house, so I go in my room at the back, read my Bible, stay out of their way, and escape the noise. The oldest child is fifteen and the only one I really talk to. The husband doesn't communicate, but the way he looks at me tells me a lot about his feelings, and they aren't good.

I don't have any choice where to live because of my fixed income. I don't drive anymore, so my granddaughter brings me most of what I need. I am in good health, but I didn't plan my last days to be like this.

Is there anything you can think of to do about it? What would you do in my place? There's a lot I'd like to tell my family, but they're not interested.

A.   Busy young families and a fast-paced society take a heavy toll on relationships today. You are not the only senior in this unfortunate and sorry situation. The key to a brighter future for you may begin with the last sentence of your letter to me: You wrote, *"There's a lot I'd like to tell my family, but they're not interested."* Here's an idea for you:

Invite your fifteen-year-old great-grandchild into your room and ask if he or she will help you on a project. You will need a tape recorder with a microphone and some cassette tapes. Spend time talking into the tape recorder about your family history, including dates, important events, births, deaths, and your feelings about them. Start as far back as you can, and have a good time with it. Recall the good times, but don't leave out the bad. Keep a happy spirit, free of blame, as you tell about your life and the family. You may want to write some things down before you begin so you don't get offtrack or miss anything important. The tapes will be a wonderful gift to your family. You could even conspire with your great-grandchild to keep it a secret until Christmas. What a surprise it would be! I think you'll find them very interested in what you have to say and quite pleased that you did this for them.

Another thing I would do is contact my pastor. Without a car, you need to be picked up on a regular basis for church events and services. Going with older friends in their cars would be a nice break for you.

Since your health is good, see if you can't volunteer for a community activity such as working in a voting booth at election time. Can you afford your own telephone? A friend of mine is ninety, and she fills her mornings with walks and her afternoons dialing the numbers of people given to her by her pastor, people who need to pray with someone or need someone to listen to them.

Getting older has been defined as "losing your options." Reach out as best you can to be a blessing to someone else. When you do that, you will have less time to think about what you don't have and more time to be the person you really are.

God bless you.

Step-Grandparenting

Q. My daughter is thirty-three and has been raising two children, ages eleven and fourteen, by herself for nearly five years. She's going to remarry soon, and her new husband also has two children, ages twelve and fourteen. The children seem to get along fine, according to my daughter. Everything's fine, except I don't know these children, and they don't know me.

I love my two grandchildren very much, and we have a very close relationship. How do I love the new ones, and should they call me "Grandma" if they want to?

A. When an adult child marries someone with "ready-made" children, you have primary and secondary grandchildren. The trick is not to make them feel that way but to treat them as equally as possible.

Parents can be leery of new grandparents coming into their child's life in a second marriage, even fearful of "grandparent games," such as playing favorites with one and ignoring another. Acceptance is important in any child's life, certainly in the new environment of a blended family.

Children want to belong, and they need to be loved, but they know when the feelings are real and when they're put on.

Step-grandparents have a unique chance to make a difference in a child's life. The outcome of their efforts depends on how their branch on the family tree is bent to accommodate the new twigs. Here are some guidelines:

1. Give the relationship time. Don't pretend you love the child instantly. Maybe you will, maybe you won't. God will bless you with an honest feeling, and the child will respond in kind.

2. Understand mood changes. The child may harbor deep feelings of resentment, fear, or concern about how he or she will be received by extended family members who are strangers. Such feelings can come out in a variety of ways. Remember, the mood swings have little if anything to do with you and everything to do with their new life and the uncertainty of the future. You may also see changes in your primary grandchildren as they jockey for position in the family and seek out their comfort levels.

3. Be interested enough to listen. Step-grandchildren need someone who cares enough to hear them out. It may take a while, but it will be worth the wait. Patience and silence make for golden moments. Without them, precious gems of information can be lost. You've heard the expression, "Once burned, twice shy." Step-grandchildren won't come back if they feel or imagine that you don't really care, and primary grandchildren need to know they can still count on you for their special needs.

4. Create happy situations in which all of the children can be themselves: a picnic, a walk in the woods, or a trip to the mall for an ice cream cone. The key here is to let everyone be themselves. The rest will come along in time.

5. Respect the wishes of the parents. This is their new family. Your job is to support them with prayer, demonstrated love, and patience. They need you, but they need you to honor their privacy and their authority.

6. Affirm your love for your biological grandchildren often. Let them know your undying grandparental devotion hasn't changed one iota.

Every child is unique before God. Step-grandchildren need all the honest-to-goodness love they can get. Love each one as Christ loves you. Let them call you anything they want. If it's "Grandma," add another ruby to your crown and shout, "Hallelujah!"

Foster Grandchildren

Q. I don't have any grandchildren. Do you have any tips for me as I enter into the new world of foster-grandparenting? Our daughter and son-in-law have no children of their own and have just been licensed for foster care. They have taken in a young brother and sister from a sad background of domestic violence and abandonment. We don't know how long we'll have them, and I'd like to make a difference in these children's lives if I can.

A. My hat's off to your daughter and her husband. Today there are roughly 600,000 children living in foster homes, and many more are waiting. The needs are great for willing hearts and homes.[5]

Foster kids won't expect to get you. All they are really looking for, hoping for, is a safe place to be, even if it isn't the place they should be and probably long for, with the people who once loved them but no longer can or no longer care. It's a scary time for them, and getting a real live grandparent is a bonus in their lives.

Kaleidoscopic emotions rage in foster children depending on the circumstances that brought them to this point. When you meet them, try to blend in to the foster family unit rather than stand out. Bring something for them the first time you are together. Keep it simple and meaningful—a small toy, or a game you might play together. Young children, especially, will respond to such a loving gesture when it also means you spend time with them.

Be ready for rejection; it may last as long as you have the relationship. Again, it depends on what they've been through. You can support the foster parents by making yourself available as respite caregiver, counselor, mediator, and comforter.

The most important gift you have to give to a foster grandchild is your faith. Demonstrating your Christian beliefs by what you say and do in the foster child's presence can make a difference in who that child becomes. Contented, well-adjusted adults who were shuttled from foster home to foster home in their youth will testify that they would not be the people they are today except for a foster-grandparent who modeled Jesus Christ for them.

Adopting a Grandchild

Q. Our grandson is six. We've had legal custody of him since he was twenty months old. He is in school now, and people are asking questions about his parents, who were totally irresponsible. Even though he calls us Grandma and Grandpa, we have been his parents most of his life. My husband is taking early retirement, and we think the best thing for our grandson would be to adopt him so we can put him on our insurance and in our wills. We think it would also give him a sense of security because he's going to get questions all through school. Do you have any suggestions for us? And how much should I tell him about his parents?

A. Your letter reminded me of an encounter I had as I paid for merchandise at a department store a couple of years ago. The salesperson and I were talking about grandparents who raise their grandchildren when the young woman in line behind me, heard our conversation. She said, "Excuse me. My grandparents raised me. They adopted me. They gave me their name and gave me an identity. I belonged. I'm thirty-three years old, and I know I wouldn't be who I am except for what they did for me."

Adoption is the most secure custody arrangement for custodial grandparents and for the child. For those grandparents who have, if you can imagine, gone to court against their own child for the welfare of a grandchild, it means the end of the haggling and the court appearances and the beginning of peace of mind. Like the stranger who spoke up in the department store, to the child it means everything.

By virtue of the adoption, the child has the right to inherit from the grandparent or his relatives just as if the child were the birth child of the grandparent. After a decree of adoption is entered, the birth parents of the adopted child are relieved of all parental responsibilities for the child and cannot exercise or have any rights over the adopted child or the child's property.[6]

On the matter of what to tell an adopted grandchild about his parents, here is advice from Jeffrey R. LaCure, a family therapist and founder of Adoption Support and Enrichment Services in Framingham, Massachusetts, and coauthor of a new book, *Raising Our Children's Children:*

> Sometimes what is said is not as important as how it is said. I never recommend that adoptive parents tell their children that "Your birth parents loved you so much they gave you to us" because its implications can be confusing and even painful. For example, an adopted child may be confused as to how someone who "loves" them so much can give them away. Also, the adopted child may wonder, "If you love me, will you give me away too?" It is far more useful for grandparents to share with their grandchildren that "Your birth parents made a decision because they cared about what happened to you. Our love and commitment means you are staying with us. Our decision means you will always stay."[7]

If you go ahead with the adoption, be sure to consult a good adoption attorney. Talk at length with your grandchild about the process. Make it a journey you take together. Consider participating in some therapy sessions with a qualified counselor to prepare both of you for what the future holds. Listen closely to your grandchild, and listen to your own hearts. Be realistic about your ability to do all that you want to do.

Love is the motivator for grandparents who adopt their grandchildren. Be as sure as you can that love will sustain you through all of the parenting stages and beyond.

Raising Grandchildren

Raising Grandchildren

HUSH LITTLE BABY

Hush little baby, don't you cry.
Gramma's gonna pray you a bright blue sky.
And if that bright blue sky turns gray
Gramma's gonna pray you a brand new day.
And on that day your life will be
All the Lord can give through me.
So hush little baby, don't you cry.
Jesus loves you and so do I.

IRENE ENDICOTT

THE RIGHTS GRANTED TO GRANDPARENTS by state law determine the degree of influence they can have in a grandchild's future. Millions of grandparents are today finding themselves in the unenviable position of seeking those rights, sometimes as the very life of the child hangs in the balance.

Parenting again, working with attorneys, suffering with or without social service workers, and navigating the system are all part of one of the saddest legacies of the twentieth century as the *grand* has been taken out of *grandparenting* for millions of grandparents.

This firestorm of our time, poignantly illustrated by the questions in section 11, was ignited by the instability of young moms and dads, including dire circumstances surrounding their moral choices or their untimely deaths.

Christian grandparents who rely on steadfast faith survive second parenthood far better than others. Please pray with me that God will continue to love His children and continue to undergird loving grandparent caregivers with His strength and His peace.

PARENTING ALL OVER AGAIN

Raising Grandchildren

Q. My wife and I are raising two grandchildren because their mom went off with somebody else, and our son is not capable. We are in our sixties. Is there help available, and how can we cope with the demands of caring for young children at our age?

A. According to the U.S. Census Bureau, approximately 3.2 million children under the age of eighteen are living with their grandparents or other kin, a 40 percent increase since 1980.[1] Some experts say the figures are much higher. You are among them, and yes, there is help for you.

Aid for Families with Dependent Children (AFDC) provides payments based on the child's income. This is not charity. It is a state-mandated payment specifically for the care of a minor child. Food stamps are available based on the household income. Some states recognize grandparents as foster care providers and offer financial assistance. Call your local Department of Social Services to see if you qualify.

Under Medicare and most medical insurance policies, your grandchildren will not be covered. Call your insurance agent to see if your private insurance policy might be one that will cover them, and if so, what steps need to be taken to make your grandchildren dependents. Also, contact your local community health clinic or physician's office to see if they provide Medicaid benefits for Early Periodic Diagnosis, Screening, and Treatment (EPDST), which is a wellness program for children.[2]

If you need help getting the children enrolled and settled into school, contact the principal of your local elementary school for answers to academic, emotional, and psychological problems you may face. You should find caring people there.

Trying to cope with the demands of two little ones, twenty-four hours a day, will wear you out. Call your local social services or child welfare office for child care assistance so that you and your wife can get away from time to time. Remember that young parents do that. You probably remember when you did that yourself.

Call on family members to help you by taking the children on outings or for a sleepover. If no relatives live close by, consult your church, or the YMCA/YWCA day-care programs.

Join or start a grandparent support group. Nothing is so affirming of the lifesaving work you are doing than to join with others in the same situation. Coming together regularly with other grandparents who are parenting all over again will be a wonderful time of sharing encouragement and resources. There are over four hundred such groups now meeting in the United States. If you do not know of an existing group, call the AARP Grandparent Information Center, which was established in September 1993, in Washington, D.C., to provide a referral source and other assistance to grandparents who are raising their grandchildren. Call (202)434-2296 on weekdays from nine to five, eastern standard time. A recorder will take your message, and someone will call you back. Or you may write the Center at 601 I Street NW, Washington, DC 20049. They can tell you if a support group meets in your area.

You are not alone in this great work. Please do not hesitate to reach out. Help and hope is available.

Helping a Grandchild in School

Q. My husband and I raised four children and are now grandparents parenting a fourteen-year-old step-grandson who was being raised in a violent home in which his mother was killed by his father. He's a good kid, but he has many problems. He is quiet and withdrawn, which is certainly understandable after all he's been through. We have him in counseling, and he's coming along fine there. He's been introduced to new friends at our church and seems to enjoy Sunday school. It's his public school that we are concerned about.

It was hard enough for him to change schools at his age, but then the kids began to tease him about his size. (He's small for his age and quite pale and thin.) They call him "ugly duckling" and "twerpy." They are relentless about it, creating situations in which our grandson looks like the culprit. He responds by lashing out, which gets him in trouble with the principal, and then we get a call. How can we help him deal with peer pressure, build his self-esteem, and help him succeed in school?

A. It's a shame that your grandson has endured such pain, loss, and changes only to be ridiculed when he needs friends. Reach back in time to when you were a parent because that, of course, is what you are to your grandson. These are some of the coping skills you will recall and that will benefit you both:

- Be involved with his teachers day to day, week to week. Tell them some of the background information that has led to the boy's quiet, withdrawn attitude and emotional turmoil. Often teachers are more compassionate if they have some facts to clarify what is happening and will become an ally or partner for parenting grandparents. A sensitive teacher can make a great difference anytime, but especially now, in the life of a vulnerable teenager who has already experienced enough hurt for a lifetime.
- Keep the line of communication wide open with your grandson. If he doesn't respond to physical touch, and he may not, take time to sit with him, take walks with him, trying to draw him out with strategic silences and patience. Over time, he will feel safer with you, tell you more, and take your advice and counsel.

- Concentrate on and encourage his strengths. Those tasks he does well, those classes in which he excels, those special interests he shows in sports, music, or any other subject should be applauded. Tell him that he may have to work harder, but he can do it. Keep your expectations realistic. You can't ask for more than his best effort. With your coaching, he will realize his value and be able to establish his place, not only in your family but at school with his peers. Being good at one thing can eclipse a hundred bad memories for a teen. Encourage him to do his best at something he really enjoys.

- Find a good role model in the extended family—an uncle or a cousin who will interact with your grandson and be a confidant and good friend. Professional counseling is very helpful, but your grandson really needs a friend too. The youth pastor at your church would be a great choice or referral source.

Let me encourage you in what you are doing. You are truly saving a life. You are a buffer between your grandson and his insensitive, cruel peers. You are a patient, caring parent who is undoubtedly sacrificing your own dreams for the future of a child. With God's help you will succeed in helping your grandson succeed in school and in life.

The Blessings

Q. I want you to know that not all grandparents who are raising their own grandchildren are unhappy about it. We have had our grandson, now eleven, since he was two. We are in our late fifties, and it has been a joy to watch my husband with this child. When we were raising his father, who is a drug addict and now in prison, my husband was building a business and had little time for his son. With our grandson, he has more time and is more relaxed and attentive to the child's needs. Although he won't discuss it with me, I think there is quite a bit of guilt on his part, stemming from his parenting years, which might be one reason he is enjoying our grandson more.

When we first took permanent custody, well-meaning friends told me I would find my schedule restricted now and wouldn't be able to do the things I wanted to do in my fifties and sixties. Well, that just hasn't happened. Our grandson is bright, independent, strong-willed, and loving. He respects us and loves us, and he knows we love him. He's the best thing that ever could have happened to us at this time in our lives, and we thank God for him!

A. Fear and trepidation can be heaped on grandparents raising grandchildren by the best-intentioned people. I know many grandparents who feel as you do. However, the great majority of those doing this lifesaving work are beleaguered, losing their life savings, sometimes their good health, and finding themselves caught in tangled and emotional dramas starring social workers, attorneys, and their children.

Guilt about mistakes that were made during the parenting years is a big issue for some grandparents who parent again. For some, it is reinforced by the system, spoken or implied: "You raised a drug addict. How can you be trusted to raise this child?" Grandparents who recognize, perhaps too late, that they could have done a better job as parents, often convert their guilt into positive action for the sake of a grandchild. If that is the case with your husband, you would do well to convince him to pour out his feelings to a professional counselor.

I'm delighted for you both that raising your grandson is such a bonus in your lives. May you be further encouraged by this unsolicited letter written by a nineteen-year-old grandson to his grandmother:

Nona,

On July 31, 1983, you unexpectedly became a mother again. You took an eight-year-old boy into your home and treated him like he was your son, as if it was normal.

Your life was turned upside down. You lost the most precious thing in the world to you—your daughter. In the middle of your pain and suffering, you found the time to take care of a scared, confused, and uncertain little boy who had just lost his mother.

As the little boy got older, he learned how to push your buttons. He had a knack for making your day miserable. Making life hard for you was his way of saying he didn't want another mom. He did everything he could to push you away, but you wouldn't leave him alone. The more problems he caused, the more you were there for him, getting him out of trouble and pushing him to do something with his life. You never thought twice about helping him when he needed it. When he was sick, you nursed him back to health. When he wanted a ride to a friend's house, you took him there. You always tried your hardest to make him happy. Now he has grown up and understands the sacrifices you made for him.

Nona, this little boy is a very grateful young man now, and I want you to know how much I appreciate all you've done for me. I want you to know that I'm proud to be your grandson. Most of all, I want you to know that I love you.

Kevin [3]

(Kevin is the nephew of nationally-known, pioneering grandparent advocate and coauthor of *Grandparents as Parents: A Survival Guide for Raising a Second Family*, Sylvie de Toledo of Culver City, California. Following the suicide of his mother, Kevin was raised by Sylvie's mother and father.)

ACTIVE GRANDCHILDREN

Raising the Busy Grandchild

Q. At age fifty-four, I'm raising a four-year-old grandson who is very active. He doesn't have any real problems; he's just busy. I guess I had forgotten how it is at this age. I get tired and frustrated. Sometimes I want to throw in the towel, but I don't because the baby would end up in foster care, and I love him so much. I saw a poem you wrote that really spoke to me and what I'm going through. Could you please send it to me?

A.   It's a prayer written by an anonymous grandparent to help her cope. Here is the prayer and God bless you.

> Give me patience when little hands
> Tug at me with small demands
> Give me gentle words and smiling eyes
> And keep my lips from hasty, sharp replies.
> Give me always a loving touch
> For the sake of those I love so much.
>
> Anonymous

The Superactive Grandchild

Q.   I am raising my nine-month-old granddaughter following her abandonment by my irresponsible and selfish daughter. I've had the baby almost all of her life and hope to adopt her. She's a happy child, but she is never calm or relaxed. As far as we know, there was no drug abuse during the pregnancy.

It's almost impossible to snuggle her. She wiggles around when I pick her up, wanting to get down again and crawl. That lasts a few minutes, then she wants to be picked up again. Before I know it, she is straining to get down again. The only time she relaxes is when she has her bottle. Nothing interests her for very long at all. She cries in her crib, only falling asleep because she's exhausted. It's hard to take her anywhere because she cries and strains in the car seat, even when the car is moving.

She's really a darling baby, very bright and beautiful. It's been a long time since I mothered a baby, and I wonder if I'm raising a potentially hyperactive child.

A. Your answers may lie in one of several possibilities: (1) There was indeed some type of drug abuse during the pregnancy that is at the root of the tension, short attention span, and crying. It may not be serious but should be checked out with a pediatrician immediately. (2) Something in her diet may be causing her behavior; that can also be determined at the doctor's office. (3) This could be a phase, perfectly normal for her age group, that will pass in time as she becomes a toddler, and her world gets bigger.

If it is simply a phase, here are a few suggestions from Marguerite Kelly who wrote *Family Almanac:*

> The Superactive Child will need a wide variety of toys that keep her interest as her abilities grow, like an activity box on her crib, blocks, balls, and wheel toys she can move. Divide her toys into two baskets and bring only one out at a time. That way, the second basket seems new.
>
> Don't always give in to her demands. Slow her down with a gentle bath after supper. Water soothes at every age. Rub her back at bedtime. Sing a lullaby. If she yells when you leave, wait about five minutes and go back, reassure her, pat her back briefly and leave. You'll do that five times in a half hour for the first few nights before she falls asleep but she will learn how to manage for herself when she finds out she can count on you to come back.[4]

Contact a local community college, YWCA, or your city health department for free reparenting classes for grandparents. You'll feel more comfortable after a refresher course on such issues as behavior, nutrition, potty training, and the big *D* word—*discipline.* It sounds like you're going to need that one!

CHALLENGED GRANDCHILDREN

The FAS Grandchild

Q. I'm raising my teenage granddaughter and recently saw a television program that scared me half to death. It was about adopted children who appear to be perfectly normal but have lost faculties because the mother consumed alcohol during the pregnancy. It was called Fetal Alcohol Syndrome, and just about every symptom they talked about, my granddaughter has. She is fifteen, and she was adopted by my daughter who was killed in a terrible accident last year. I am at the end of my rope with her behavior. There has to be some kind of answer because I'm doing my best for her. What can you tell me about Fetal Alcohol Syndrome, and do you think she has it?

A. Fetal Alcohol Syndrome (FAS) is the number one known cause of mental retardation in the nation. The American Medical Association reports that the rate of FAS births in the year 1993 (6.7 per 10,000 births) was more than sixfold higher than that for 1979.[5]

Fetal Alcohol Syndrome is caused by maternal alcohol abuse during pregnancy. When a pregnant woman drinks alcohol, it reaches the baby within a few minutes. Prenatal exposure to alcohol, especially in heavy doses, causes irreversible brain damage and lifelong disabilities including facial abnormalities.

FAS children show central nervous system disorders such as poor coordination, hyperactivity, attention and learning problems, and developmental delays. Some, but not all, have lower IQs.

Alcohol has been suspected as a cause of prenatal damage since biblical times. Judges 13:7 says, "Behold, thou shalt conceive and bear a son; and now drink no wine nor strong drink" (KJV). In early Carthage, there was reported to be a prohibition against the bridal couple drinking on their wedding night for fear of producing a defective child. In 1834, a report to the British House of Commons said: "Infants of alcoholic mothers often have a starved, shriveled, and imperfect look."[6]

Babies with full FAS are below average in height and weight. They typically have thin upper lips and short noses with low bridges. The area between the nose and lips is long and smooth. Their eye slits are small, giving the appearance of wide-set eyes.

Adoptive parents who were not able to examine the birth record and parent history of their child sometimes discover some baffling behavior patterns and are at a loss to know which way to turn. Most doctors don't have the specialized training to detect a specific set of symptoms. I recommend that you contact The Fetal Alcohol Syndrome (FAS) Family Institute, P. O. Box 2525, Lynnwood, WA 98036, for more information.

Can you see the adoption file? You may not have an FAS granddaughter, but it is worth checking out. There is nothing to be done to reverse the damage of FAS, but there are new support organizations that can help parents cope with this heartbreaking syndrome, a condition that would not exist had the mother abstained from alcohol during pregnancy. A nationwide effort is now under way to stop the consumption of alcohol by expectant mothers.

The Dyslexic Grandchild

Q. My neighbor told me to write to you about my great-grandson who is ten and having quite a bit of trouble in school. He's a boy who has been through many things that should never happen to children. Both of his parents were on drugs, and they abandoned him when he was eight. I got him from social services when he was living alone on the street, and now I have legal custody. I am sixty-eight.

He is slow with most things, although I don't push him. He fails in reading, and his other grades are poor even though he works hard at his studies. He is healthy now and has lots of friends, so it's hard to understand why he's not doing better in school. My neighbor thinks he has dyslexia. I suppose it could be so. What should I do about that?

A. *Dyslexia* is not a scary word. Some experts estimate that one out of every seven schoolchildren have dyslexia, others say that up to 30 percent of all schoolchildren have it, with a conservative estimate of 7 percent having it severely. So, that should be comforting for you.

I suggest you contact the Orton Dyslexia Society, 724 York Road, Towson, MD 21203, 1-800-222-3123 or the Learning Disabilities Association of America, 4156 Library Road, Pittsburgh, PA 15234, for information so you can make an informed decision about testing your grandson for dyslexia.

Recent findings indicate that dyslexia or SLD (Specific Language Disabilities) are likely to appear in reading, spelling, speaking, handwriting, and composition. Do any of the following characteristics seem familiar?

- Difficulty in learning and remembering printed words
- Poor ability in visual recall of well-studied words
- Confusion about directions (left, right, up, down)
- Reversals of some letters (b, d, p, g) or the order of letters in words (saw, was; quite, quiet)
- Left-handedness
- Poor ability to reproduce a rhythm in sequence by tapping
- Speech disorders such as poor sentence construction
- Cramped and illegible handwriting
- Persistent spelling errors
- Poor ability to associate sounds[7]

Ask your school principal to assist you in getting your grandson tested. He's been through a lot and may just be learning delayed, but you'll feel better knowing the facts, and he will have a better chance of succeeding in school and in life once his learning problems are defined.

When Mother Is in Prison

Q. My daughter was arrested and sentenced to prison for six years. She is in a prison about sixty-five miles from my house.

I have guardianship of her four-year-old child, my grandson. He's a handful. There is no father. I'm sixty-two and not as young as I used to be.

I spent many years trying to keep my daughter out of trouble and helping her make something of herself. She has thanked me with a life of bad choices that have landed her where she is. My main concern is protecting my grandson. I have a temporary guardianship. There's going to be a hearing soon, and I am considering whether I should file for permanent custody. My attorney says that, considering my daughter's record, I should. I'd appreciate any information you can give me on my choices in this matter.

A. Grandmothers are increasingly called upon to act as parents for grandchildren because the children's mothers are increasingly being incarcerated. An estimated seventy-five thousand grandmothers may face this circumstance before the decade concludes, and thousands more will be called upon for similar aid while their adult daughters serve on probation or parole or struggle with incapacitation from drug abuse.[8]

Your short-term guardianship is just that: a legal custody arrangement for a limited period of time. Guardianship is always temporary. Even if your grandchild has lived with you since birth, the court can revoke your guardianship status. Remember, the prevailing belief is that children belong with their parents. However, while parents can request the court to overturn a guardianship arrangement, they must prove that they can care for the child and that continued guardianship is no longer necessary. This is rarely accomplished when the problem is substance abuse.[9]

Legal custody would give you more control over whether your grandchild is handed back to an abusive or neglectful parent. Without it you may have problems enrolling a child in school, getting medical care, or seeking government aid.[10]

Ask your attorney to carefully explain to you the various forms of custody and how the law in your state applies to your situation. Then you can make a fully informed decision about the future of your grandson.

Emotional Blackmail

Q. I received my two little granddaughters four months ago from my daughter, who is divorced from a very abusive young man. She receives AFDC money, but I haven't seen any of it since she left to go live somewhere else, just dumping the kids here with me. I don't have an attorney or any other help. I am a widow on a fixed income, which is barely enough for me. I hear from my daughter about once a month. She asks about the kids but never tells me when she's coming back for them.

I'm afraid to call the authorities for fear they'll take the girls away into foster care and I'll never see them again. Is there anything I can do? This is too much for me!

A. This is a particularly difficult situation of emotional blackmail. Your daughter is off on her own, still receiving money from the system while you parent her children!

According to Mary Fron, founder and president of ROCKING, Inc. (Raising Our Children's Kids: an Intergenerational Network of Grandparenting), a grandparent in this dilemma can wait patiently for the parent to come to a sense of responsibility *or* ask the family court for *emergency custody*. Such an action would give you a legal standing until a formal custody hearing could be held and may result in the AFDC (Aid to Families with Dependent Children) funds being diverted to you, the caregiver. That should get some reaction from your daughter.

Only you can make this choice. From ROCKING, Inc., here are some questions to ask yourself:

- How long am I willing to live this way?
- Can I live this way for five days, five years, or indefinitely?

- What is the worst thing that could happen if I refuse to be "blackmailed" any longer?
- What is the best thing that could happen if I refuse to be "blackmailed" any longer?
- Can I live with the possible consequences of refusing to be "blackmailed" any longer?
- What can I do to regain control of my life?[11]

WORKING WITH THE SYSTEM

How to Hire an Attorney

Q. I have just received my granddaughter, age three, from Children's Services. She was found abandoned by my daughter, who is divorced and involved with drugs. I know as soon as she can, my daughter will come for the child, but I do not want to allow my grandchild back into that terrible lifestyle. I need an attorney and don't know the first thing about getting one to help me.

A. When looking for an attorney, a grandparent should insist upon someone whose practice emphasizes family law and *someone who has experience representing grandparents in third-party issues.* Since custody, visitation, and adoption of grandchildren by grandparents is a relatively new phenomenon in American courts, screen potential attorneys for that specific experience.

Do not look in the phone book! Ask for personal referrals or contact a lawyer referral service in your area. Your state's bar association has a lawyer referral and information service.

When you have all of your questions answered and are comfortable with an attorney's competence, decide whether or not you can work with the individual you hope to hire. Is he or she concerned about and attentive to your problems? Does he or she believe in your case? Is this person capable of effectively advocating for your position? The attorney is your employee. You are entitled to ask questions regarding background, experience, continuing education, and special third party experience. (Some attorneys are reluctant to work with certain state agencies.)

Most attorneys will want an advance retainer before taking your case. In giving your attorney a retainer, you are merely prepaying for so many hours of time, depending on the hourly rate. If your case settles early on or if for any reason you should drop the case, find out whether (and how much of) your retainer is refundable.

Ask if there is a qualified attorney in the firm who works *pro bono* (free of charge). Some attorneys donate their time for the public good.

Good communication between you and your attorney is critical. When you meet for the first time, be prepared with facts, recorded information, and dates. You may be asked to keep a diary.

Hourly rates of attorneys may vary anywhere from $80 per hour to $175 and up, based on experience. You will pay more for an experienced attorney, but often that attorney can accomplish the work in a shorter amount of time. In other words, a higher hourly rate may not necessarily result in a substantially higher bill. In this field, *there is no substitute for experience.*

What Is Kinship Care?

Q. We are raising two grandchildren under ten years of age, and it is tough financially. AFDC money doesn't go nearly far enough to care for these children. We've heard of something new called kinship care that might make foster-care money available to us. What is kinship care, and how do I know if we qualify?

A. *Kinship care* is the term usually applied to relative caregivers. You may be referring to the Kinship Care Act of 1995, that would help grandparents in their role as caregivers by allowing states to provide services and assistance to relatives in lieu of foster care payments to people outside the child's family.

The author of the bill is Representative Ron Wyden of Oregon. *The assistance would be available only for children who have been removed from their parental homes and for whom court action has been taken.*

In kinship care placement, the state would transfer custody of the child from foster care to the adult relative; then the state would have the flexibility to make some payments or provide services to the child under existing foster-care programs. The bill also would require participating states to monitor the progress of children and families as well as the children's safety. After four years, the Secretary of Health and Human Services would evaluate the results and recommend legislative changes to Congress.[12]

If you received your grandchildren after removal from their parental home in a court action, contact your local office of DHHS for more information.

Cooperating with Social Services

Q. When my daughter died, the state gave me custody of her two children. I am on a fixed income, and it is very difficult to take care of all of the needs of growing children, ages seven and eight. I have had three different social workers assigned to me in the year I have had the children. I've never been so discouraged in my life! I thought they were supposed to help! The first one was rude, told me to stop complaining, and threatened that the children might be taken away. The other two did not check on us once. When I called them, they did not follow through with answers to my questions. I'm not even sure of the name of the current one. That could be because I just try to do everything myself now and keep them out of it. It's not worth the hassle. How can I get the help I need?

A. The plain truth about the state social service systems is that there are some poor workers, and some very able workers who are overworked and underpaid. Often they have so many cases that they couldn't possibly service all of them well.

Sometimes the system is *too* involved, which can have extremely negative repercussions for grandparents who want the best for their grandchildren. The horror stories are legendary.

You obviously were assigned poor workers, and I can't blame you for trying to handle things by yourself. I have these suggestions for you: Remember that a social worker doesn't work for you but for the best interests of the child. A social worker's main ambition is to return the child to custody of the parent, if at all possible. They are trained to think unemotionally and legally.

Sylvie de Toledo, founder of the organization Grandparents As Parents, has written a book with Deborah Edler Brown that is *must* reading for every grandparent who is raising a grandchild. The title is *Grandparents as Parents, A Survival Guide for Raising a Second Family*, published by Guilford Press. In it, de Toledo advises:

> Be nice to social workers. Use understanding. Tell specific facts. Remember that not every social worker who disagrees with a grandparent is a bad social worker. Not every child who cannot be with his parents should be with his grandparents. There are grandparents who really should not have their grandchildren because of health, medical, or psychological problems. Some children may be better off in a foster home if there is no other relative to take them.[13]

Make sure you have good legal representation on which you can rely for help, both immediately and long-term. A good attorney will help you sort out your financial situation and help you make the decisions that are right for you and right for the child.

Child Protective Services and You

Q. We are a Christian family with a long heritage of generations of commitment to the church and to each other. We have had that mold broken for us by the marriage of our daughter, her husband's drug use and physical abuse, their subsequent divorce, and our fear for the very life of our granddaughter who is just three years old. We have had our granddaughter for three months, since our daughter disappeared without any warning. We don't know where she is and whether she will ever return.

Our granddaughter first was placed in protective custody, then placed with us. We thought our troubles were over, that we could provide a good life for this child until Child Protective Services stepped in. Since then, we have been living a nightmare.

They threaten. They come unannounced and ask ludicrous questions about our home life. They make us feel like they want to take our grandchild away from us and put her into foster care. Do we have any defense?

A.   Once Child Protective Services gets into the picture and juvenile court takes over, you and your grandchild are locked into the system. Decisions are taken out of your hands and are placed in the hands of the court. Make certain you have an attorney experienced in family cases who understands your situation and will work diligently for you and the future of your grandchild.

At present, Child Protective Services (or whatever name child protection services are called in your area) is under severe scrutiny. A number of states have passed laws diminishing the power of this state agency or are getting to the bottom of neglect and abuse by the system that has caused, in some instances, the death of a child. Activist groups are lobbying for new safeguards against the abuses by some Child Protective Services staff.

Having visited grandparent support group meetings around the country, I have heard more ranting and raving from grandparents about child protection services than any other problem they deal with as they parent their grandchildren. The reorganization or outright abolishment of social services must become a priority with state legislatures across the country!

You need a good attorney—*now*.

"We must bring the child back to the center
of our care and concern. This is the only way
that our world can survive because our children
are the only hope for the future.
As older people are called to God,
only their children can take their places."

Mother Teresa
(National Prayer Breakfast, Feb. 3, 1994)

COPING

Starting a Support Group

Q. There are several of us in our neighborhood who have had various problems with our children and who now have our grandchildren. We have checked and cannot locate a nearby support group. What are some guidelines for starting our own? I know others would come.

A. If you are raising a grandchild or are embroiled in a visitation conflict or working on a possible adoption, you can enjoy the companionship and encouragement of others in similar situations. It's easy.

Inquire at your church, your doctor's office, local hospital, clinic, or social service agency for free space available on a regular basis. When you have located space for your meetings, make up a simple flyer or notice to post in the church, clinic, or agency, or perhaps to be publicized by a hospital auxiliary. If necessary, place a small ad in the newspaper announcing that grandparents caring for grandchildren are meeting at a certain place and time. People should come because statistics show the needs are great.

At the meeting, keep it simple. Say hello, pass around a sign-up sheet so you can keep in touch with everybody by mail and phone, and ask who would like to speak first. You'll find that people will begin talking almost immediately, sharing stories, problems, and resources, even before the meeting convenes. One of the great benefits of support group meetings is finding another person who is experiencing a situation similar to yours.

From time to time, invite a special speaker, such as an attorney, a child advocate, a judge, or a CPS worker who would speak, then answer questions. Ask those attending to bring to the next meeting any newspaper or magazine articles that might help someone else and display them on a table during the meeting.

If you decide on a more formalized structure for your meetings, be sure to leave plenty of time for informal discussion, because that's when much of the real help is offered and gladly received.

If you ask for a dollar from each person attending, you may be able to do a monthly or quarterly newsletter.

July and August are good months to substitute the regular meeting with a picnic at a grandparents' home where their grandchildren can meet each other and other extended family members for a time of enjoyment.

Your group can become a nonprofit organization by creating a board of directors and registering with the Secretary of State. Be sure to register your group with the AARP national grandparent center by calling (202) 434-2296. God bless you!

The Power of Prayer

Q. This is hard to summarize, but I'll try. I have a son who is in prison for life on murder charges and a daughter who tricked me for years about her drug habit. I had to quit my job with two years to go before retirement to raise their small children. Instead of a promotion, I have commotion. Instead of looking forward to travel and leisure, I look forward to diapers, potty training, and parent-teacher conferences. I have given up on asking why; I'm into *how?* And I've never spent so much time in prayer in my entire life.

Without prayer, I could not survive. When it all gets to be too much, I sit down and talk to God. I just talk to Him like I'm talking to you. He knows how much I can take and lifts the weight off my shoulders. I don't have anybody else to talk to, who could give me peace about my kids, peace to put my own life on hold, and peace to do my best for these grandkids. They didn't ask for what has happened to them, and they look to me like I look to God.

At night, I open my Bible, and it's like a light shining up at me with the answers. My favorite verse in Isaiah 54 says, "Do not fear for I am with you." I read that, and I start to pray and everything's all right again. I give the *why* to Him and He shows me the *how.*

A.   Turning to God is our best hope for coping with the demands and pressures of raising a grandchild. Meredith Minkler and Kathleen M. Roe are two doctors who have studied the power of prayer in the lives of second-time parents. In their book, *Grandmothers as Caregivers, Raising Children of the Crack Cocaine Epidemic,* they cite the responses of those who have witnessed the power of prayer:

> He sent me a vision and I started praying . . . And that's what turned it around. For a long time, I was praying the wrong prayer. I was praying for her. Lord, keep her safe, Lord, help her quit, Lord, take care of her . . . And then one day I said Lord, take her, but give me the strength to go on. And that turned it around.[14]

> Sometimes I go to bed at night and I say "I don't care if I never get up in the morning." And then, the next morning, the Lord just pushes me right out of bed and says, "You're not through yet." And I get up stronger.[15]

For some grandparents, just getting up in the morning is enough work to do. For the grandparent who also wakes up each day to do somebody else's work, the nights are shorter, the days far longer. Prayer is the leveler, God's instrument of grace that enables us to go on. God bless you in this lifesaving work.

Epilogue

I MET WITH TWO GRANDMOTHERS, strangers to each other, on a park bench. Neither was experiencing the grandparenting season they had anticipated and earned. The one on the left sat with hunched shoulders, spoke haltingly as she spilled out her sorrow to me, and intermittently wiped her eyes, reddened by an unstoppable river of tears—justifiable tears—for herself, for her family, for lost hopes and dreams.

The one on the right was well acquainted with such grief, for her family was also going through difficulties with outcomes yet to be learned. She sat still, at peace, as she outlined the sorrowful repercussions of her children's choices, her eyes still moist from tears long ago shed at the foot of the Cross.

Both grandparents had asked to speak privately with me, but they did not need me. I watched as the one on the right lovingly reached out her hand to the other. This one who was suffering just as much as the other, but who exuded an extraordinary aura of peacefulness and compassion, gently took the other's quivering hand, held it ever so softly in her own, leaned forward to her and said, "Will you pray with me?"

I was privileged to watch the miracle of faith flow from a believer to a seeker. I saw the peace that passes all understanding come over the grandmother on the left during what might have been her first conversation with the Lord. As the three of us took turns praying, I could feel strength pouring into the grandmother on the left as she unburdened herself to the Lord. At the amen, the one on the left had dry eyes, a big smile, and a new resolve to trust God. She had placed her family in His hands.

The circumstances of their grandparenting season were similar. The difference in the grandmothers was *faith*. They needed each other, and they needed Jesus Christ. He was there for them both.

Whether you, dear reader, stand on the mountaintop of joy as a grandparent or in a valley of despair, I hope you will seek out another with whom you can share. Most of all, seek Jesus. The power of faith in our loving, merciful Lord will bless you mightily and sustain you today and into the unknown future.

Ask your questions of Him in prayer. Wait. He will answer and give you His peace.

Questions for Meditation and Prayer

Do I have a good understanding of God's gift of grace and what it means in my grandparenting season?

How am I modeling Christ to my grandchildren?

How am I faithfully praying for my grandchildren?

What is my role in the family?

Is there an area in my relationships with my children and grandchildren that needs forgiveness?

Am I repeating the generational sins of my past?

How am I being "dumped on" by my children or grandchildren?

How have I ever crossed the line from healthy concern to meddling?

Am I enabling my adult child to continue in bad habit patterns?

Do I clearly understand my responsibilities in giving and loaning money?

What legacy will I leave? Will it be temporary or eternal?

Erma Bombeck's Job Description for Grandparents

A grandparent can always be counted upon to buy anything you're selling, from all-purpose greeting cards to peanut brittle, from flower seeds to cookies, from transparent tape to ten chances on a pony.

A grandparent buys you gifts your mother says you don't need.

A grandparent will put a sweater on you when she is cold, feed you when she is hungry, and put you to bed when she is tired.

A grandparent will frame a picture of your hand that you traced over the brocade sofa in the Mediterranean living room.

A grandparent is the only baby-sitter who doesn't charge money to keep you.

A grandparent will believe you can read when you have the book upside down.

When a grandchild says, "Grandma, how come you didn't have any children?" a grandparent will fight back the tears.

Thank you, Erma. We will miss you.

Notes

Introduction

1. U.S. Department of Health and Human Services, *Morbidity and Mortality Weekly Report* 43 (26 August 1994): 609.
2. Irene M. Endicott, *Grandparenting by Grace: A Guide Through the Joys and Struggles* (Nashville: Broadman & Holman, 1994), 6.
3. Selma Wilson, editor, *Journey* (Nashville: Southern Baptist Convention Sunday School Board, June 1996), 1.

Section 1

1. Eugenia Price, as quoted in *A Working Woman's Guide to Joy*, compiled by Gwen Weising (Bloomington, Minn.: Garborg's, 1995), week 14, Wednesday.
2. Judith Waldrop, "The Grandbaby Boom," *American Demographics* (September 1993), 4.
3. Rachel Pruchno, Ph.D., "Grandparents in American Society" (National Institute on Aging, September 1995): 1.
4. Louise Wollman, *The 1990s Grandmother* (White Plains, N.Y.: Peter Pauper Press Inc., 1990), 18–19.
5. Dorothy Sickal, *Hands across the Seasons* (Alexandria, Ind., Gaither Family Resources, 1988), 94.
6. Dr. Paul Faulkner, *Achieving Success without Failing Your Family* (West Monroe, La.: Howard Publishing Co., 1994), 32.

Section 2

1. Marguerite Kelly, *Marguerite Kelly's Family Almanac: The Road to Good Manners* (New York: Simon & Schuster, 1994), 197. Adapted.

Section 3

1. Roberta C. Bondi, *To Pray and to Love: Conversations on Prayer with the Early Church* (Minneapolis: Fortress Press, 1991), 138.
2. Johnny V. Miller, "He Showed Us How to Pray," *Decision*, January 1996, 13.
3. "Praying for and with Your Grandchildren" (Bethany, Okla.: Prayerlife, 1993).
4. William J. Bennett, *The Devaluing of America: The Fight for Our Culture and Our Children* (Colorado Springs: Focus on the Family, 1994), 131.

Section 4

1. Dr. Dan Montgomery, "A Grandparent's Grace," *Grandparenting* February 1996, 14.
2. Sam Goldstein, Ph.D., "Sibling Rivalry" (CH.A.D.D., February 1996), 11-13.
3. Ibid.

Section 5

1. Karen O'Connor, *Restoring Relationships with Your Adult Child* (Nashville, Thomas Nelson, 1993), 167–70.
2. Judith Balswick with Lynn Brookside, *Mothers and Daughters Making Peace* (Ann Arbor, Mich.: Servant Publications, 1993), 11.
3. Susan Raborn, "When Church Bells Aren't Ringing," *Focus on the Family* January 1996, 3.
4. Vicki Elaine Legg, "Twelve and Holding," *Home Life*, May 1996, 55.

Section 6

1. Jerry Bridges, *The Practice of Godliness* (Colorado Springs: NavPress, 1983), 214.
2. Isabel Wolseley, "Love Letters," *Guideposts*, March 1994, 13.
3. Stephen J. Bahr, "Trends in Child Custody Awards," *Family Law Quarterly* 28, no. 2 (Summer 1994): 247.

Section 7

1. Charles H. Spurgeon, *The Blessings of His Love: Morning and Evening* (Nashville: Thomas Nelson, 1994), entry for May 20.
2. Billy Graham, *Hope for the Troubled Heart* (Word), as quoted in *Reader's Digest*, March 1995, 178.

Section 8

1. Fay Angus, as quoted in June Cerza Kolf, *Grandma's Tears* (Grand Rapids: Baker Books, 1995), 22.
2. Kelly, *Family Almanac*, 522–523.
3. Irene M. Endicott, *Grandparenting by Grace: A Guide Through the Joys and Struggles* (Nashville: Broadman and Holman, 1994), 156.
4. Kolf, *Grandma's Tears*, 18.
5. Annie Johnson Flint as quoted in Ruth M. Sissom, *Moving Beyond Grief* (Grand Rapids: Discovery House, 1994), 29–30.

Section 9

1. Benjamin Franklin as quoted in Billy and Janice Hughey, *A Rainbow of Hope* (El Reno, Okla.: Rainbow Studies, Inc., 1994), 128.
2. Matthew Soska, "How to Enable Children to Live a Drug-Free Life," ACCESS ERIC (Educational Resources Information Center, Rockville, Md., March 1995).
3. The University of California, "Passive Smoking" *Berkeley Wellness Letter* 10 (August 1994): 7.

4. Mary Fron, *Empowerment of Grandparents* (Niles, Mich.: R.O.C.K.I.N.G., Inc., 1994), 4.

5. *Morbidity and Mortality Report*, 609.

6. National Coalition Against Domestic Violence, P.O. Box 18749, Denver, CO, 80218.

7. Michael Medved, as quoted in Ronald A. Reno, "Before Our Very Eyes: What TV Sex and Violence Are Doing to Us," *A Focus on the Family Report* (1995): 1.

8. Ibid.

Section 10

1. Susan Lenzkes, *No Rain, No Gain: Devotions to Guide You Through the Storms of Life* (Grand Rapids: Discovery House, 1995), 36.

2. Ibid., 36.

3. Traci Truly, *Grandparents' Rights: Should You File for Custody?* (Clearwater, Fla.: Sphinx, 1995), 25–26.

4. Ibid., 15.

5. "America's Children at Risk," *Family Law Quarterly* 27, no. 3 (Fall 1993) 441.

6. Lauri Hanson, Browne Lewis, and Connie Booth, LICSW, "Grandparent Resource Manual" (Legal Aid Society of Minneapolis, 1995), 15–16.

7. Deborah Doucette-Dudman with Jeffrey R. LaCure, *Raising Our Children's Children* (Minneapolis: Fairview Press, 1996), 42.

Section 11

1. Doucette-Dudman and LaCure, *Raising Our Children's Children*, 1.

2. "Grandparents Raising Their Grandchildren: What to Consider and Where to Find Help" (Washington, D.C.: AARP, 1993), 4–5.

3. Sylvie de Toledo and Deborah Edler Brown, *Grandparents as Parents: Survival Guide for Raising a Second Family* (New York: The Guilford Press, 1995), 274.

4. Kelly, *Family Almanac*, 182.

5. "Fetal Alcohol Syndrome Trends," *The Journal of the American Medical Association* 273 (May 1995), 1.

6. *Manual on Adolescents and Adults with Fetal Alcohol Syndrome*, U.S. Department of Health and Human Services, 1988, 3.

7. Betty Ruckhaber, "A Parent's Discussion of Dyslexia" (Towson, Md.: Orton Dyslexia Society, 1995).

8. American Society on Aging, "Children of Women Prisoners," *Generations* (Spring 1996): 39.

9. de Toledo and Brown, *Grandparents as Parents*, 153.

10. Ibid., 144.

11. Fron, *Empowerment of Grandparents*, 5.

12. "AARP Perspectives: Transfer of Custody," *Modern Maturity*, February 1996, 86.

13. de Toledo and Brown, *Grandparents as Parents*, 183–84.

14. Meredith Minkler and Kathleen M. Roe, *Grandmothers as Caregivers: Raising Children of the Crack Cocaine Epidemic*, (Newbury Park, Calif., Sage, 1993), 120.

15. Ibid.

Resources

AARP Grandparent Information Center
601 E Street NW
Washington, DC 20049
(202) 434-2296 (9:00-5:00, EST)

Grandparenting by Grace (Church Study Course)
Discipleship & Family Development Department
Sunday School Board, Southern Baptist Convention
127 Ninth Avenue North
Nashville, TN 37234
(615) 251-3900

Grandparents as Parents (GAP)
P. O. Box 964
Lakewood, CA 90714
(310) 924-3996
(310) 839-2548 FAX (714) 828-1375

United Grandparents Raising Grandchildren (UGRG)
2019 N.E. 12th Street
Renton, WA 98056
(206) 271-3397

Grandparents Raising Grandchildren, Inc.
20227 87th Avenue West
Edmonds, WA 98026
(206) 774-9721

Grandparents United for Children's Rights

137 Larkin Street
Madison, WI 53705
(608) 238-8751

Raising Our Children's Kids: An Intergenerational Network of Grandparenting (R.O.C.K.I.N.G., Inc.)

P. O. Box 96
Niles, MI 49120
(616) 683-9038

Grandparent's Rights Organization (GRO)

555 South Woodward, Suite 600
Birmingham, MI 48009
(313) 646-7191

Children and Adults with Attention Deficit Disorder (CHADD)

499 NW 70th Avenue, Suite 109
Plantation, FL 33317
(305) 587-3700

National Committee for the Prevention of Child Abuse

332 South Michigan Avenue, Suite 1600
Chicago, IL 60604
(312) 663-3520

National Information Center for Children and Youth with Disabilities (NICHCY)

P. O. Box 1492
Washington, DC 20013
(800) 695-0285

Mothers Against Violence in America
901 Fairview Avenue North, Suite A-170
Seattle, WA 98109
(800) 897-7697

Lutheran Social Service
2485 Como Street
St. Paul, MN 55101
(612) 774-9507

Mothers Against Drunk Driving (MADD)
511 E. John Carpenter Freeway, Suite 700
Irving, TX 75062
(214) 744-6233

Prison Fellowship
P. O. Box 17500
Washington, DC 20041
(703) 478-0100

American Bar Association
Center on Children and Law
740 15th Street NW
Washington, DC 20005
(202) 662-1000

BOOKS FOR GRANDPARENTS

Biehl, Bobb and Cheryl. *Pre-Remarriage Questions* in the *Heart to Heart Series*. Nashville: Broadman and Holman, 1994.
de Toledo, Sylvie and Brown, Deborah Edler. *Grandparents as Parents: A Survival Guide for Raising a Second Family*. Guilford Press, 1995.

Doucette-Dudman, Deborah with LaCure, Jeffrey R. *Raising Our Children's Children*. Fairview Press, 1996.

Dunzer, John. *Grandfather's Handbook: How to Understand and Have Fun with Your Grandchild*. Great Times Press, 1995.

Endicott, Irene M. *Grandparenting by Grace: A Guide through the Joys and Struggles*. Nashville: Broadman and Holman, 1994.

———. *Redefined: Guidance for Today's Changing Family*. Lynnwood, Wash.: Aglow Publications, 1992.

Gaither, Gloria, ed. *365 Meditations for Grandmothers*. Dimensions for Living, 1994.

———. *Hands across the Seasons*. Alexandria, Ind.: Gaither Family Resources.

Kelly, Marguerite. *Marguerite Kelly's Family Almanac*. Fireside, Simon and Schuster, 1994.

Minkler, Meredith and Roe, Kathleen M. *Grandmothers as Caregivers: Raising Children of the Crack Cocaine Epidemic*. Sage Publications, 1993.

Moore, June Hines. *You Can Raise a Well-Mannered Child*. Nashville: Broadman and Holman Publishers, 1996.

O'Connor, Karen. *Restoring Relationships with Your Adult Children*. Thomas Nelson, Inc., 1993.

Poe, Lenora Madison, Dr. *Black Grandparents as Parents*. Self, 1992.

Schreur, Jerry and Jack. *Creative Grandparenting: How to Love and Nurture a New Generation*. Discovery House Publishers, 1992.

Sherrer, Quin with Ruthanne Garlock. *How to Forgive Your Children*. Lynnwood, Wash.: Aglow Publications, 1989.

Stoop, Jan and Southard, Betty. *The Grandmother Book: Sharing Your Special Joys and Gifts with a New Generation*. Thomas Nelson, Inc., 1993.

Index

About the Author

Irene Endicott is one of fifty-nine grandchildren whose grandmother gave birth to seventeen children. One of eleven children, mother of four, step-mother of three, grandmother of fourteen and great-grandmother of one, Irene is sixty-two-years-old.

She was a columnist for *Grandparenting* magazine, a Thomas Nelson publication, is a consultant on grandparenting issues to the Sunday School Board of the Southern Baptist Convention, and serves on the national committee for Women's Enrichment Ministries. For ten years, she hosted a live radio program for women and families on Christian broadcasting in Seattle, Washington. She is a nationally known speaker, conference leader, and a staunch advocate of grandparents in legal and social services arenas. Irene is the author of four books on the subject of grandparent-ing, a book editor, and writer of children's stories and numerous articles, and is quoted widely on the subject of grandparenting. She lives on Puget Sound in Washington state with her husband of thirty years, Bill, who is also a writer.

You are encouraged to write Irene with your questions or comments.

Irene Endicott
P. O. Box 350
Hansville, WA 98340

242